TRUTHBETOLD

BASICS IN CATHOLIC APOLOGETICS

LIFE TEEN

The information contained herein is published and produced by Life Teen, Inc. The resources and practices are in full accordance with the Roman Catholic Church. The Life Teen® name and associated logos are trademarks registered with the United States Patent and Trademark Office. Use of the Life Teen® trademarks without prior permission is forbidden. Permission may be requested by contacting Life Teen, Inc. at 480-820-7001.

Cover design by David Calavitta.
Interior design by Nick Heller and Laura Womack.

Authored by Mark Hart and Joe Cady.

Copy editing by Natalie Alemán and Katie Oertle.

Special thanks to all those who have contributed to this piece in its original form.

ISBN: 978-0-9853575-2-8

Copyright ©2012 Life Teen, Inc. All rights reserved.

Published by Life Teen, Inc.
2222 S. Dobson Rd.
Suite 601
Mesa, AZ 85202
LifeTeen.com

Printed in the United States of America.
Printed on acid-free paper.

For more information about Life Teen or to order additional copies, go online to LifeTeen.com or call us at 1-800-809-3902.

TABLE**OF**CONTENTS

THE BIBLE

THE CHURCH

SACRAMENTS

SIN AND SALVATION

THE POPE

MARY AND THE SAINTS

INTRODUCTION

BY MARK HART

Archbishop Fulton Sheen once said, "There are not over a hundred people in the United States who hate the Catholic Church. There are millions, however, who hate what they wrongly believe to be the Catholic Church." He understood something many "intellectuals" seem to miss about the Catholic faith, namely that the Roman Catholic Church (and, by extension, everything the Church teaches) is far more than it appears, and it is deeply misunderstood by countless people.

The Church is misunderstood, primarily, because it is not just a building or a corporation. The Church is not a "what" as much as it is a "who"; the Church is our Mother. Like any good mother, she feeds us (Sacraments), teaches us (doctrines), guides us (Magisterium), and shows us how to live rightly (the Saints). The Church is further misunderstood because sin makes people suspicious about the "why", as in "why does the Church teach this or that?" If we doubt the purity of the Church's mission (the "why"), we will doubt her instructions for the mission (the "what" of her teachings) along the way.

Put another way, if you don't trust in your earthly mother's love, then rules, chores, and curfews all seem more like forms of control or punishment rather than means to develop character, responsibility, or virtue.

So what is the answer? Is the Church supposed to just be silent? Is "mom" just expected to shut her mouth and sit idly by while her children make destructive decisions that will cost them their lives? Is that really good for a child? Is silence in this way an act of love? Is this "tolerance" toward poor behavior really the highest form of respect? Or is it the deepest form of irresponsibility?

The sooner that we recognize the Church as our Mother and not just an institution, the quicker we realize that – like any mother – she wants what is best for us. Why? Because she loves us. While we, as children, may not necessarily like everything she says (or how she says it) at times, we know and trust that she says those things for our own good. Our Mother Church wants us to live, to be joyful, and to be free. That's what truth does: it frees us (John 8:32).

In the end, Mother Church deals with three kinds of children: saints, brats, and runaways. Saints are still sinners, but they are sinners who are open to truth and the transformative power of God's grace. Brats can assuredly become saints but only after their hearts and minds are open to Christ. Runaways (those who flee from the Church) can become saints, too, but only after they stop running from accountability and they embrace truth and acknowledge that there is a God and it's not them. In fact, some of the greatest saints in our Church's 2000 year history began as runaways and countless spent a better portion of their lives as brats.

This book is not designed to offer an exhaustive explanation to every facet of Catholic teaching. This is a starting point – not a finish line. There are dozens of topics not covered here. What we've tried to do, however, is cover the most foundational questions about Catholic teaching and some of the most frequently misunderstood. Many of these answers you may already "know" or agree with but struggle to explain in everyday conversation with family and friends. We answer each question in two ways: "In Brief" and "In Depth."

The "In Brief" answers are for when you need a quick response to a deep question. They allow you to share the foundation of a longer answer, with enough information to satisfy someone until you have time to really have a discussion. For some souls you encounter, the short answer will suffice. It will demonstrate that the Church is logical in what she teaches and sums up our beliefs in a concise, one-minute explanation.

The "In Depth" answers are designed for longer conversations. They will walk you more into the "why" of Church doctrine, beyond just the quick facts. This section will draw more from Scripture and the *Catechism of the Catholic Church* to demonstrate the framework and progression of thought behind certain teachings. Further, the "Suggested Reading" sections will offer *Catechism* references, Papal writings, and solid Catholic books you can check out to go even deeper on specific topics. There is also a "Things to Consider" section that can be found in some sections that has useful quotes from Scripture and Church documents to aid you in your study of Catholic Apologetics.

Our hope is that this book whets your appetite to study and share even more. The Church may be beautifully misunderstood as that first quote reminded us, but she is still beautiful. Christ established the Church (as you'll read more about) because He knew we would need it and because He loves us.

Open your heart as you turn this page. Ask the Holy Spirit, who is the Source and Guardian of the Church, to continue to guide you – and all of us – to truth (John 16:13)... a truth that needs to be shared, a truth that needs to be told.

EXISTENCE **OF** GOD

HOW DO WE KNOW THAT GOD EXISTS?

IN BRIEF:

We can know that God exists by considering the simple concept of *cause* and *effect*. We all know that every cause has an effect, but this of course means that every effect must also have a cause. Now, when we look at the physical world and ask ourselves where everything came from, we come to recognize the basic truth of reality; things don't just zap themselves into existence. Everything that exists in the world (whether a shoe, a car, a tree, or a person) is an *effect* that is caused to exist by something outside of itself. Nothing brings itself into existence or causes its own existence. Everything that we experience in the world is an effect of something else. But if we stop and think about it, we realize that this chain of causes cannot go back indefinitely; at some point we must admit that there has to be something that is the reason for everything else existing in the first place. There must be a "*first cause*," and this first cause is God.

IN DEPTH:

This is one of those questions that people have wrestled with for many centuries. It is related to a bunch of other questions that we often ask ourselves like where did we come from and what exactly are we doing here? The answer to the question of God's existence is extremely important if we are going to answer any of the other questions found in this book. So, what's the answer? How can we know that God really exists? Well, some of the greatest minds in history have attempted to present arguments for God's existence, many of which are based upon the idea of *cause* and *effect*.

St. Thomas Aquinas, one of the most brilliant theologians in the history of Christianity, said that when we look at the world, we see that **Nothing that we experience in the world is the cause of itself.** everything that exists is caused to exist by something outside of itself. Nothing that we experience in the world is the cause of itself; everything that we see can only be explained by some cause outside of itself. Take, for example, a cell phone. Now, no one in their right mind would claim that cell phones cause themselves to exist. Obviously they are made by someone or something, and are therefore *caused* to exist by something other than themselves. But let's be irrational for a minute and pretend that the cell phone *did* cause itself to exist, that all the pieces of the phone came together on their own to form the phone. We would still be left with a problem because one important question would remain: Where did all the pieces come from? In answering that question, we would discover that the pieces came from a factory that makes cell phone parts. But where did the factory come from? Did it just happen to form over the centuries? Of course not! Someone had to have made it. (Everyone, I hope, would agree to this.) But if we keep going backward, asking where the thing before it came from, we are still left with a question: What caused any of this to exist in the first place?

Without a cause there can be no effect.

Everything we encounter in the world is an *effect* of some other thing (which is that thing's *cause*). Without a cause there can be no effect. As we go back looking for the causes of all the things that we see in the world, at some point we realize that the chain of causes cannot go back forever. It is impossible for the list of causes to go on to infinity. At some point we have to admit that there must be a *first cause* that got the ball rolling in the first place because without a first cause, none of the other effects would be possible. This first cause must be something whose existence is not dependent upon something outside of itself. In other words, the first cause must be self-existing; it must be *existence itself*. This self-existent first cause is what we call God, who is existence itself and the cause of everything else that exists. This truth about God as "being" or "existence" is beautifully contained in the name that God reveals for Himself to Moses: "I am who I am" (Exodus 3:14). God *IS*. He doesn't have existence; He is existence. He isn't one being among many beings; He is *being itself*. It is the very nature of God *to be*.

Let's look at this from another angle as well. When we look at everything that exists, we see an incredible amount of order and complexity. Consider again a cell phone; not only do we have to admit that it came into existence by some cause outside of itself, but we must also acknowledge that whatever or whoever caused it to exist must be pretty smart. Because of the complexity of the cell phone, we recognize that whatever caused it to exist must have done so with an intelligent design in mind. Someone didn't just start gluing and screwing pieces together. It was put together with precise parts in exact locations, knowing that only then would it function properly. This is true of everything we see.

Let's consider something even more complex, like the human body or the Universe; not only does its very existence lead us to conclude that there must be some first cause that explains how it got here, but its intricate order and complexity also lead us to conclude that it must have been caused to exist by some *intelligent designer*. When we come to see the complex nature of creation and the way all of its parts function in such a well ordered manner, we are led to acknowledge an intelligent designer as the cause of its ordered design. In short, the beauty and wisdom of creation is a reflection of the intelligence of God, the Creator, who is wisdom itself.

When we come to see the complex nature of creation and the way all of its parts function in such a well ordered manner, we are led to acknowledge an intelligent designer as the cause of its ordered design.

The important point to see is that the existence of God *can* be known by looking at the world itself. We don't have to turn to the Bible to try and prove God's existence. We merely need to look at creation and we will see evidence of a creator who is both wise and powerful. St. Paul affirms this in his letter to the Romans: "Ever since the creation of the world, [God's] invisible attributes of eternal power and divinity have been able to be understood and perceived in what He has made" (Romans 1:20). The question of God's existence begins to be answered when we start asking the question, "Where did we come from?" What we find is that none of us are here by our own power; everything that exists is dependent upon something else for its existence. There must be a first cause that explains the existence of everything else in the world. This first cause is God.

SUGGESTED READING:
CCC 31-38
St. Thomas Aquinas, *Summa Theologica*, First Part, Q. 2, A. 3
Peter Kreeft, *Because God is Real*, Chapter IV

IF GOD EXISTS, WHY IS THERE SO MUCH EVIL IN THE WORLD?

IN BRIEF:

Evil in the world is the result of our *free choice* to disobey God and act in ways that are harmful and destructive. Our free will was given to us because God wants us to freely accept His love and share in His goodness. But when we use our free will to choose things that are against what is right and good, evil results. God does not desire or will evil. (The phrase "will evil" means to cause or intend evil for its own sake.) He desires only what is good. But He does allow evil to exist because, mysteriously, He is able to bring about good from it. Jesus Christ, who used death itself as a means to bring us new life, reveals this in a beautiful way. Sin and evil do exist, but God is bigger than them, and He can bring about good even through the mess that our disobedience has made.

IN DEPTH:

Not having a good answer to this question is probably the biggest roadblock that keeps people from believing in God. It is usually referred to as the *problem of evil*, and the line of reasoning usually goes something like this: If there really did exist an all good, all powerful God, then surely He would and could prevent so much evil from occurring in the world. Therefore, since there is evil in the world, God must not exist. This is a legitimate question and it is one that needs to be addressed. As we answer this question, it is important to keep one thing in mind: we are not going to deny that there are many instances of evil and suffering in the world. You only need to flip on the news to see that evil is real. So, no one is denying that there *is* evil in the world. What we are attempting to do is answer this important question: Does the existence of evil in the world prove that God does not exist, and if not, why not?

In order to answer this question we have to first look at what evil actually is. We have to keep in mind that God is goodness itself, and all that He has made is good.

"For you love all things that exist, and detest none of the things that you have made, for you would not have made anything if you had hated it."

- Wisdom 11:34

God doesn't create evil, He wills and creates *only* what is good. So we shouldn't think of evil as a *thing*, but rather as the *absence* of a thing — the absence of good. Evil is the lack of a good that should be there. For example, murder is evil because it is the lack of care for the life of another. Stealing is evil because it is the lack of proper respect for what belongs to others. Lying is evil because it is the absence of truth. Life, property, and truth are all goods that we need in order to develop into who God made us to be. When those things are absent or denied through the actions of others, that is evil. What is important to realize is that God is not the cause of evil, especially in these cases. It is free human actions that bring about evil. It is by *not* seeking and doing what is good that evil (the absence of a good) exists.

> **We shouldn't think of evil as a thing, but rather as the absence of a thing — the absence of good.**

Now, someone might say that since God made the people who do evil, He is responsible for their evil actions. It is true that God made all of us, but He made us with free will, and *this freedom is a good thing*. Our freedom was not given to us so that we could do whatever we want with our lives; it was given to us so that we could freely choose what is good and experience the fullness of life as God intends it. So often, in our world, freedom is thought of as a free ticket to do anything we want, but this is a sad misunderstanding of what freedom is really for. God made us free so that we could freely accept the love that He wishes to share with us. Our freedom is only properly exercised when we freely choose what is good. With this freedom (which is good and is meant for good) comes the ability to make destructive choices, choices that manifest a lack of good and therefore cause evil.

> **It is true that God made all of us, but He made us with free will, and this freedom is a good thing.**

So then, why didn't God just program us to always do what is right and good all the time? Well, God could have created beings like that, but they wouldn't be human beings. They would be robots, internally programmed to act in pre-determined ways. And what would be the point of that?

When two people get married, they express their vows to one another—their *free commitment* to love each other completely and faithfully for the rest of their lives. Part of what makes this commitment so special is the fact that of all the women in the world, the man chose to unite himself to this particular woman, and of all the men in the world, she chose to commit herself to this particular man. She wasn't programmed to love him. She chose to love him, and he chose to accept her love and freely return it. Realizing that this love is freely given and freely reciprocated is what makes love so special. Now, let's say that instead of this free choice, he had somehow programmed his wife to love him and be faithful to him. Would this really be love? Would she really understand his love and devotion to her? Could he really say that she had given herself to him? Of course not! Well, in a similar way, God is love. And out of love He desires to share with us His own life and goodness. But He wants us to recognize this as a great gift and to freely respond to it with faith and loving trust. He doesn't want programmed robots who can't actually understand the greatness of the gift they have been given; He wants free beings to love, people who will realize just how amazing God's love is and will freely choose to accept it. This is where free will comes in. With this freedom comes the ability to make choices contrary to the love and goodness God intends for us.

It is important to recognize that God desires only good things for His children.

God is good. He never wills evil. However, He does allow it, "Because He respects the freedom of His creatures and, mysteriously, knows how to derive good from it" (*CCC* 311). The problem of evil is no easy question to address. It is important to recognize that God desires only good things for His children. He lovingly cares for His creation, guiding it according to His purpose of uniting all things to Himself and allowing us to share in His own life and goodness. Evil exists in the world because through sin and disobedience, we have *chosen* to turn away from what is good and do what is contrary to God's will. But God, in His wisdom and love, is able to use even sin and evil to bring about good. This is most profoundly seen in the death and Resurrection of Christ, through which God was able to use the suffering of His own Son to bring about the redemption of the world and give us access to new life in the Spirit.

Evil is nothing that we should take lightly, but inspired by our Faith, we must recognize that goodness will always have the last word. Even though we might not always be able to explain why a particular evil has taken place, we must be confident in the fact that God's love is greater than sin.

As Mother Teresa said, "Never let anything so fill you with sorrow as to make you forget the joy of the Risen Christ." [1]

SUGGESTED READING:

CCC 309-314, 1730-1738
Peter Kreeft, *Because God is Real*, Chapter XV

THINGS TO CONSIDER:

> *"From the greatest moral evil ever committed – the rejection and murder of God's only Son, caused by the sins of all men – God, by His grace that 'abounded all the more,' brought the greatest of goods: the glorification of Christ and our redemption" (CCC 312).*

---

1   Mother Teresa, *Life in the Spirit*, 63

WHY DO WE CALL GOD "FATHER"?

IN BRIEF:

We call God "Father" because that's what He told us He is. In the Old Testament, God is understood as the Father of the people of Israel and of all creation (see, for example, Psalm 89:27). And then in the New Testament, Jesus repeatedly refers to Himself as the Son of God and shows us that God is Father not only because of His loving care for all that He created, but because He is eternally the Father of His only begotten Son. While God is rightly understood in the Old Testament as a father in that He made us, cared for us, and guided us on the right path, the great truth of the New Testament is that God is Father in a very real sense because Jesus is truly the Son of God (see John 5:17-18), and because God offers us adoption as His own children (see 1 John 3:1-2). (The relationship between the Father and the Son will be looked at more closely on page 9).

IN DEPTH:

For those who are Christian, calling God "Father" might seem like a very normal and natural thing. Consider, for example, how many times you have prayed the *Lord's Prayer* throughout your life, or how many times you have begun a prayer "In the name of the Father..." But where does this practice come from, and what exactly do we mean when we refer to God as "Father"?

Even though referring to God as "Father" is most commonly associated with Christianity, this practice actually existed prior to the coming of Christ. In the Old Testament, the Israelites referred to God as Father for a variety of reasons. God was understood as Father because He was the Creator of all. Just as a child has life from and through his or her parents, the Israelites understood that the world had life from and through God. Therefore, calling God "Father" emphasized His parental care for His creation. It also served as a reminder of the fact that all creation is ultimately subject to the authority of God. For the Israelites, God was Father because of His relationship to what He created.

However, there is another reason why the Israelites understood God as Father. One of the central themes of the Old Testament is the fact that God chose the Israelites to enter into a unique relationship with Him. From among all the nations of the world, God chose to form a covenant with the people of Israel. To the Israelites alone, God reveals His law with the hope that they would function as a light to the Gentiles. It was God's desire that, through the holiness of Israel, all nations might recognize the God of Israel as the one true God. Because of this unique role, Israel was referred to as God's "first-born son" (Exodus 4:22). Therefore, by calling God "Father" the Israelites drew attention to the unique relationship that they had with God.

Despite all of these reasons for calling God "Father" in the Old Testament, with the coming of Jesus, God is revealed as "Father" in an entirely new way. At the heart of Jesus' message was the fact that He was sent by the Father for the purpose of doing His Father's work. Now this was, in a certain sense, true of the prophets in the Old Testament as well; they were called and sent forth by God with a message that came from God. But Jesus makes claims that no prophet before had ever made. He said things like, "No one knows the Father except the Son and anyone to whom the Son chooses to reveal Him" (Matthew 11:27). "The Father and I are one" (John 10:30). "Whoever has seen me has seen the Father" (John 14:9). In each of these statements Jesus is showing us that He has a unique relationship with God the Father. This relationship is so intimate that Jesus can say that He and the Father are one, and that He knows the Father in a way unlike anyone else.

Now, while the details of this relationship will be covered more fully in the next question on the Trinity, for now it is important to realize that when Jesus speaks of God as Father, He is not calling to mind some general notion of God as Creator; He is showing us that God is Father precisely because He has a Son — a Son who is eternally begotten (or born) of the Father, and who was sent into the world to fully reveal the Father to all the world. This is why Jesus can say, "Whoever has seen me has seen the Father" (John 14:9). Jesus is the Son of God who became man so that, through faith, we might also come to share in the life of God as adopted children of the Father. Christians call God "Father" because Jesus revealed to us that His Father is also our Father.

SUGGESTED READING:

CCC 232-248
Mark Hart, *The "R" Father: 14 Ways to Respond to the Lord's Prayer*

THINGS TO CONSIDER:

The Israelites are God's chosen people in the Old Testament. The Israelites consisted of the 12 tribes of Israel (the descendants of the 12 sons of Jacob).

Calling God "Father" indicates that He is "the first origin of everything and transcendent authority, and that He is, at the same time, goodness and loving care for all His children" (CCC 239).

A covenant is a sacred agreement between two people or groups. In a covenant, each party is bound by certain obligations, and rewards or punishments are given based upon faithfulness to the demands of that agreement.

"Jesus revealed that God is Father in an unheard-of sense: He is Father not only in being Creator; He is eternally Father in relation to His only Son, who is eternally Son only in relation to His Father" (CCC 240).

HOW CAN GOD BE "THREE IN ONE"?
WHAT IS THE TRINITY?

IN BRIEF:

The Trinity is the belief that God a "communion of persons": Father, Son, and Holy Spirit. These divine persons are distinct from one another, but at the same time, they are all totally one in the divine nature. God is one, but He is not solitary. Throughout the centuries saints and writers have tried to explain how the Holy Trinity can be one and, at the same time, three. St. Patrick used a three-leaf clover to show the distinction. You could also look at it this way: consider a fire, which consists of flame, heat, and light. All of these aspects or elements of the fire are distinct from one another, and yet they come together to form one fire. Now this analogy (like the one before) is certainly not a perfect analogy, and in fact, no example could possibly give us a full picture of how God can be three in one. Why? Because the mystery of the Trinity is far beyond anything that we experience in this life. But, the important thing for us to realize is that we don't believe this about God because we have figured it out or because our human reason tells us so; we believe this because God has revealed His identity to us. Our knowledge of the Trinity does not depend on our ability to explain or understand it; it depends upon our faith in the one who revealed it to us, God Himself. We believe that God is a Trinity not because we have discovered it, but because Jesus and the Holy Spirit have it made known to us (see, for example, Matthew 11:27, 28:19; Luke 24:49; John 14:26, 15:26, 16:12-15; 2 Corinthians 13:13).

IN DEPTH:

The first thing we need to keep in mind about the Trinity is that it is not something that we have figured out on our own. It's not as though people looked at all the evidence and considered all the arguments and then said, "Well, yeah, of course, God must be a Trinity." No, this is something that we believe based upon the authority of God who has revealed it. We believe that God is a Trinity because that's what He told us. Back in ancient times, many people believed in multiple Gods. When the Jews said they believed in "one God," that was very different. When Jesus came onto the scene and introduced one God in three persons, people really began to scratch their heads, so the Church (led by the Spirit) gave us a hand in understanding it, like she does with all confusing theological questions.

So, what exactly is the Trinity? The dogma of the Trinity states that God, in His very essence, is a communion of persons, Father, Son, and Holy Spirit; all one in the divine nature, but distinct in their relationship to one another.

What? Come again? If you are having trouble wrapping your mind around this, don't feel bad; some of the most brilliant minds in history have had the same difficulty. But let's see if we can break this down a bit.

First of all, we believe in one God, not three Gods. God is one; there is one divine nature (or substance, or essence, these words are sometimes used interchangeably). But, within this one divine nature there stands (subsists) three distinct persons: the Father, the Son, and the Holy Spirit. This distinction of persons has been explained in the following way: within the one divine essence, there are said to be two processions, the *generation* of the Son and the *spiration* of the Spirit. We know, "generation" and "spiration" are not exactly words you use often, but keep reading.

A *procession* is something coming forth from another. For example, when I speak, the words proceed from my mouth. Now, everything that exists proceeds from God in the sense that it comes (forth) from Him. But all of these things are external processions, because what proceeds from God, in these cases, exists outside of God, outside of the divine nature. Examples of "external processions" from God would include all of creation: the sun, the moon, the stars, the mountains, etc.

There are two processions, however, that are unique because that which proceeds remains within the one divine substance. These are the two internal processions of *generation* and *spiration*.

The Son is generated from the Father (or "begotten" or "born" of the Father), and the Holy Spirit is spirated (or breathed forth) from the Father and the Son. Let's take a look at both:

Jesus, the Son
The idea behind the first procession is that the Father forms an image or idea of Himself that is perfect and therefore one with the divine nature. This image (or Word or Son) of the Father is

identical to the Father in all things except one, in its relation to the Father. What makes the Son distinct from the Father is the fact that He is related to the Father by *filiation*, which is a fancy way of saying sonship. What makes the Father distinct from the Son is the fact that He is related to the Son by *paternity*, or fatherhood.

The Holy Spirit
The love and unity shared between the Father and the Son is the source of the second procession. From their love and unity, there proceeds a Spirit that is breathed forth from them both. This Spirit is identical to the Father and the Son in all things except one: its relation to the Father and the Son as having been breathed forth (or spirated) from them.

Divine Math: 1 + 1 + 1 = 1
Now, at this point, there is a really good chance that you are still lost. That's okay. The point here is that what makes the persons of the Trinity one is the fact that they are all one in the divine substance or nature. What makes them three is the unique relationships among them.

These explanations of the internal divine processions (which have been greatly simplified here) are attempts to explain how God can be both three and one, but they should never be understood as trying to prove the truth of the dogma of Trinity. We accept this teaching as true not because of the strength of an explanation, but because of the revelation that we have received from God.

In the New Testament we find Jesus referred to Himself as both one with the Father and yet distinct from Him (John 8:19, 10:30, 13:3, 14:23, 17:5), and we hear of the Spirit being sent from the Father and the Son and yet one with them (John 7:39, 14:16, 15:26). From the very beginning, the Church was confronted with what seemed like a paradox, that God is one but that there is a three-ness in Him somehow. Over time, the Church, guided by the Holy Spirit, came to define this truth in the dogma of the Trinity, which proclaims one God in three persons.

SUGGESTED READING:

CCC 249-260

Frank Sheed, *Theology for Beginners*, Chapter IV

THINGS TO CONSIDER:

A dogma is an officially defined teaching of the Church, one which all the faithful are bound to accept in faith (CCC 88).

"We do not confess three Gods, but one God in three persons, the 'consubstantial Trinity.' The Divine persons do not share the one divinity among themselves but each of them is God whole and entire" (CCC 253). Consubstantial means of the same substance or one in being.

"The Divine persons are relative to one another. Because it does not divide the divine unity, the real distinction of the persons from one another resides solely in the relationships which relate them to one another [...] Indeed, 'everything (in them) is one where there is no opposition of relationship'" (CCC 255).

WHO IS JESUS?

HOW CAN JESUS BE FULLY GOD AND FULLY HUMAN?

IN BRIEF:

Clark Kent was a superhero (Superman) dressed as a regular guy. He tried to "disguise" his superhuman nature through his exterior appearance. Bruce Wayne, on the other hand, was just a regular guy without superpowers, who dressed up like something more than he was (Batman).

Jesus isn't like either of these characters. First, Jesus is real. Second, Jesus wasn't like superman "trying to look normal and human." Jesus was completely human; it wasn't a "disguise." At the same time, unlike Batman Jesus, was not "acting super" or superior, either. Jesus was fully God at all times, not just momentarily doing feats that were beyond human ability or comprehension.

He is completely human, just like you and me (except He is sinless). Jesus is also completely divine.

In the first few centuries of Christianity, this truth about Jesus Christ being 100 percent human and also 100 percent divine was debated heavily, with many people heretically saying that He was one or the other, or "half and half." Luckily, the truth of God's dual nature (called the hypostatic union) was clarified by the Church as time went on, most specifically at the Councils of Nicaea in 325, Ephesus in 431, and Chalcedon in 451 AD.

IN DEPTH:

Jesus was "like His brethren in every respect" except sin (Hebrews 2:17, 4:15). So Jesus got stomachaches and headaches. Jesus could get sunburned and parched in the heat. Jesus had hormones. Jesus sneezed (although we don't know what people replied to Him when He did). Jesus laughed (Psalm 2:4) and wept (John 11:35). He is completely human, just like you and me (except He is sinless). Jesus is also completely divine. He walked on water, raised the dead, multiplied loaves, and cleansed the lepers. He was capable of eminently more than me or you, obviously, because He is God.

Both of these realities can occur simultaneously. During His time on earth Jesus certainly was more than met the eye, but Jesus is not a "transformer"; He did not "change" from one nature to the other. Both were constant and simultaneous and inseparably linked.

Heresies (doctrinal mistruths and erroneous opinions that contradict Church teaching) spread during the early centuries of Christianity regarding Christ's dual nature. Early on, the Gnostics sought to deny that Jesus was fully human. Later, at the Council of Nicaea, (AD 325) the Church confessed that Christ was homoousios ("of the same substance" of the Father), condemning the Arians who said Christ was "from another substance" (*CCC* 465). The Nestorians claimed that Jesus was a human "joined to the divine person of God's Son" (*CCC* 466), which is a misguided teaching that was swiftly destroyed by the piercing theological truth of St. Cyril of Alexandria at the Council of Ephesus in 431. In Ephesus, too, the teaching that Mary truly was the Mother of God was formally advanced. Still later, the Monophysites argued the Christ's human nature ceased to exist when the divinity of God's Son assumed it (*CCC* 467), yet another erroneous thought process struck down – this time – by the Council of Chalcedon in 451. The heresies kept coming in subsequent centuries and were, each time, shot down by the Church who repeatedly and consistently clarified this eternal truth of Christ's eternal union time and time again.

> **It can certainly be confusing to our normal human intellect and faculties to envision God's divine mind existing "within" and powering a human brain, as would be the case with Christ.**

It can certainly be confusing to our normal human intellect and faculties to envision God's divine mind existing "within" and powering a human brain, as would be the case with Christ. The *Catechism of the Catholic Church* defines it, further, this way:

> *By its union to the divine wisdom in the person of the Word incarnate, Christ enjoyed in His human knowledge the fullness of understanding of the eternal plans He had come to reveal. What He admitted to not knowing in this area, He elsewhere declared Himself not sent to reveal.*
>
> - CCC 474

Take some time to pray through the following verses to see – Scripturally – where the basis of the Church's teaching on this subject comes from (Mark 8:31, 9:31, 10:33-34, 13:32, 14:18-20, 26-30; Acts 1:7).

It's important to note, too, that the Church mirrors this hypostatic union. The Church – guided and powered by the Holy Spirit – is most certainly divine. At the same time, the Church – of imperfect members, the living stones (Romans 12:4; 1 Corinthians 12:12; 1 Peter 2:5) – is also completely human.

> **It's important to note, too, that the Church mirrors this hypostatic union.**

Put very simply, God became like us so we could become like Him.

SUGGESTED READING:
CCC 466-468
Alan Schreck, *The Essential Catholic Catechism*, Chapter IV

QUESTION 6

IS IT ILLOGICAL TO BELIEVE IN THE RESURRECTION?

IN BRIEF:

The tomb was empty. It's well documented that the founders of other "faiths" are buried in tombs or had their ashes sprinkled over foreign lands. Not Jesus. Modern "scholars" and directors can claim what they want on their cable specials, but the truth is that there was no body left on that Easter Sunday; the tomb was empty. Additionally, there were post-Resurrection appearances of Jesus not only to the eleven remaining apostles, but also to *hundreds* of people. Over a span of six weeks, He appeared to a variety of groups of various sizes in different locations. He appeared to over 500 at one point – a huge number to be an outright "fabrication." Not to mention, the people whom He appeared to didn't just "see" Him, but ate with Him, walked with Him, touched Him. Jesus even made breakfast at one point (John 21:9). Modern scholars might struggle because they didn't see Jesus in His Resurrected glory with their own eyes, but we can't dismiss the testimony of countless others simply because we weren't there.

IN DEPTH:

Many people will tell you that "based on human logic," the Resurrection makes no sense. The first thing we need to remember is that "human logic" is not omnipotence. God makes it very clear that "[His] ways are not our ways, nor are His thoughts our thoughts" (Isaiah 55:8-9).

What is illogical is to think that "man" is the center of the universe. The truth is that Christianity is far more logical than many people give it credit for, certainly more "logical" than atheism or agnosticism. The complexity of the cosmos, the earth, the human body, all of these bear witness to an intelligent design, and by extension, a divine designer. The second thing we should remind people of is that any conversation about God is going to necessitate a degree of faith. If people are not willing to humbly admit that they don't have all the answers then the conversation will go nowhere. God's truth and human pride do not co-exist in the same space; that is the nature of sin. Humility and grace go hand-in-hand, as do pride and sin.

So, let's remember that any conversation about the existence of God or the truth about Christ's Resurrection necessitates a humble admission that "it is possible that God exists" and that "we are not God." When it comes to Easter Sunday, however, and the glorious truth about the Resurrection, to say that there is no logical truth to this belief is not only ignorant, it is absurd.

The truth is that Christianity is far more logical than many people give it credit for, certainly more "logical" than atheism or agnosticism

Here are some very quick facts that point to the truth of the Resurrection. These are not exhaustive or highly detailed; they are quick points that further strengthen what humble-hearted believers take on faith:

The tomb had a Roman seal and a Roman guard.
Clay was affixed to a rope (stretched across a rock) and to the tomb itself. The Roman seal was pressed into the clay. Break the seal, you break the law; break the law, you die. The "guard" was at least four men, possibly more, of highly trained soldiers. These soldiers were experts in torture and in combat, not easily frightened off by a band of fishermen and tax collectors. Had they fallen asleep or left their post, they would have violated the law, resulting in their own execution.

The tomb had a huge stone in front of it.
Most scholars put the weight of the stone at about two tons (4000 pounds), probably at least seven or eight feet high. This was definitely a "team lift" or "team roll," not movable by just one or two men.

The martyrdom of witnesses offers proof.
Would people leave their businesses, careers, homes and families, go to the ends of the earth, die horribly gruesome and painful deaths, and forsake their previous "religious beliefs about salvation" all to protect a 'lie'? Not one of them, while being beheaded, fed to lions, boiled in oil, crucified upside down or burned alive 'changed their story.' Instead, they sang hymns of trust and praise, knowing that the Lord who defeated death would raise them up, too.

The Church is still going strong.
If the Resurrection were a lie, it would have died off centuries
ago. The Christian Church is the largest institution of any kind
in the history of humanity. This Church began with the apostles
following Pentecost, the year Christ rose. It has conquered
empires, withstood attacks (inside and out), and grown in spite of
the sinfulness of its members because it was founded by Christ,
Himself, and is guided and protected by the Holy Spirit. The
Church, like Christ, is both human and divine.

Jesus, Himself, prophesied that it was going to happen.
Jesus told people that it was going to happen. It didn't "take Him
by surprise." He didn't just say "I'm going to be killed" (which
others might have seen coming), but also that "I'm going to rise
on the third day." Those details aren't ironic, coincidental, or
fortune telling; they're called prophecy and true prophecy comes
from God, Himself.

The Old Testament prophesied it was going to happen.
It was foretold centuries before Christ, Himself, was born or lived
it out. There are hundreds of prophecies about the Messiah,
what He would say, do, live, and how He would die; they were
offered centuries apart by people God selected (most of whom
never met one another, by the way). Isaiah, Jeremiah, Zechariah,
Hosea, and Micah (just to name a
few) all pointed to Christ's death
and Resurrection hundreds of years
before they occurred.

Those details aren't ironic, coincidental, or fortune telling; they're called prophecy and true prophecy comes from God, Himself.

The day of worship changed.
Following the Resurrection, tens
of thousands of Jews (almost
overnight) abandoned the centuries
old tradition of celebrating the
Sabbath on the last day of the week and began worshipping on
the first day of the week — the day on which the Lord, the Christ,
beat death, sealing the new and final covenant with God.

The practices of sacrifice changed.
Jews were always taught (and taught their children –
Deuteronomy 6) that they needed to offer an animal sacrifice
once a year to atone for their sins. After the Resurrection, the
Jewish converts of the time, throngs of them, stopped offering
animal sacrifices to God.

It is unique among other religions.
No religious leader of any consequence every actually claimed to be God except Jesus. No other religious leader ever did the things Christ did. No other religious leader ever backed up their "religious voice" with Resurrection. Confucius died. Lao-tse died. Buddha died. Mohammed died. Joseph Smith died. Christ rose from the dead.

> *No religious leader of any consequence every actually claimed to be God except Jesus.*

The message is "self-authenticating."
This proof goes back to the original point, namely, that a humble heart is enlightened and illuminated by far more than logic or reason. A true believer doesn't need all the facts to believe in the Resurrection because the Holy Spirit intimately and powerfully reveals Christ to us. St. Paul talks about this in 2 Corinthians 4. Blind and hardened hearts will never see God, not until they acknowledge that they are not Him.

The miraculous end fits His miraculous life.
You want logic? Christ healed the blind, the deaf, and the dumb. He fed the masses, cured the lepers, and forgave the sinners. He made the lame walk and brought others back to life. He multiplied food, walked on water, and calmed storms with merely His voice. The miracle of Good Friday is that He didn't call on a miracle. He died. The miracle of Easter Sunday is that He rose from the dead – a miraculous "end" to a miraculous life. What else should we expect?

Only in the Resurrection does suffering make sense.
The world cannot offer any cure for suffering. The world can ignore it, berate it, debate it, bomb it, and medicate it, but there is no cure or point to suffering separated from Jesus Christ. In Christ, our suffering has a point, and it has worth. Apart from Christ, suffering is pointless and fruitless. There is no fountain of youth. There is no miracle drug. There is no cure for death except Jesus Christ.

> *There is no cure for death except Jesus Christ.*

That's the truth, and what a beautiful truth it is (John 8:32).

SUGGESTED READING:
CCC 640-657
Peter Kreeft, *Fundamentals of the Faith*

I CAN BELIEVE THAT JESUS WAS A GOOD MORAL TEACHER, BUT HOW CAN HE BE GOD?

IN BRIEF:

Most of the greatest writers, thinkers, philosophers, and theologians have grappled with this question over the centuries. The claims made by the carpenter from Nazareth were so audacious that they demand a verdict. Put simply, either Jesus is the Son of God or He isn't; there really isn't a third option.

No other religious leader of consequence ever actually claimed to be God. Buddha, Mohammed, the Dalai Lama, Confucius, Joseph Smith, etc. all claimed to have special insight into God or to have been called by Him, but none claimed equality with God (as Jesus did), and none backed it up with miracles like Resurrection (as Christ also did). Still others, over the past four millennia, had intriguing or seemingly profound insights into God but, again, no one (minus a few quacks) ever claimed to be equal to God, except Jesus.

Given the life Jesus lived and the words He spoke, He can be called many things, but a mere "teacher" or "moral philosopher" He could not be because of the extraordinary assertions He made. He came not from a metropolis but from a small village (Nazareth), one so obscure it's not even mentioned in the Old Testament. He wasn't raised a Rabbi, yet He had a staggering intellect that left the most learned of the day speechless. He spoke with the authority of heaven, not merely as one quoting others in authority. People witnessed celestial events around Him (the Baptism in the Jordan and the Transfiguration to name just two). He performed mighty works – recorded in non-Gospel accounts and by historians like Josephus – which no one could mirror or explain. There were tens of thousands of people crucified in the ancient world, but we're still only talking about one. His resurrected body was seen by hundreds of people (which you can read more about on page 21).

Given this extraordinary nature of the evidence, it is completely illogical to reduce Jesus of Nazareth to nothing more than a great "teacher."

IN DEPTH:

Many people, even those of other faiths, have great admiration for Jesus. Some hail Him as a great moral teacher; others see Him as a champion of social justice and a hero for the oppressed. Still others look at Him as a prophet and an important, anti-institutional religious leader. While these perspectives are certainly valid, they ignore some of the most fundamental things that Jesus, Himself, said (John 10:30, Mark 14:62, John 8:58). They also ignore the miraculous events described and accounted for in The Acts of the Apostles and the explosion of growth (despite intense persecution and martyrdoms) within the early Church.

Jesus is who He claimed to be, the Son of God, or He was lying or He wasn't God but believed Himself to be (making Him a lunatic).

As the great author (and Christian) C.S. Lewis put it in his classic book, *Mere Christianity*:

> *I am trying here to prevent anyone saying the really foolish thing that people often say about Him: "I'm ready to accept Jesus as a great moral teacher, but I don't accept His claim to be God." That is the one thing we must not say. A man who said the sort of things Jesus said would not be a great moral teacher. He would either be a lunatic – on a level with the man who says he is a poached egg – or else He would be the Devil of hell. You must make your choice. Either this man was, and is, the Son of God: or else a madman or something worse. You can shut Him up for a fool, you can spit at Him and kill Him as a demon; or you can fall at His feet and call Him Lord and God. But let us not come with any patronizing nonsense about His being a great human teacher. He has not left that open to us. He did not intend to.*

This position by Lewis offers a great framework for proving the divinity of Christ. Jesus is who He claimed to be, the Son of God, or He was lying or He wasn't God but believed Himself to be (making Him a lunatic). So in this section we'll take a deeper look at all three of Lewis' "options."

Is He a Liar?

Some say that Jesus' claims of divinity were false, and that He knew them to be false, which would make Jesus an outright liar. Further, since so many of His teachings were about Himself, His identity and the desires of God, one could not merely say He was a "false teacher" but – worse yet – that He was evil. For if Jesus was not God, then His teachings were leading countless souls – many religious, devout people – away from the one, true God and straight toward hell. If Jesus was intentionally lying and deceiving people, He was the worst, most deadly teacher to have ever walked the planet.

How could someone delusional teach what He taught, debate as He did, and offer such sublime words even during persecution and intense suffering?

Is He just a lunatic?

Some would argue, though, that Jesus "believed" Himself to be God because He was delusional. They'd say that He really wasn't God but insanely thought Himself to be. Not only would that make Christ insane but egomaniacal and self-obsessed. This "vision" of Christ is completely contradictory to the Gospels. How could a lunatic speak with such clarity and authority? How could a crazy person develop and maintain such a loyal following, even after His death? How could someone delusional teach what He taught, debate as He did, and offer such sublime words even during persecution and intense suffering? Why would His apostles and other disciples continue to follow Him and spread the news of His Resurrection if He had, indeed, died and proven Himself no more than a (dead) man?

Is He the Lord?

This leaves us with the self-authenticating truth that Jesus Christ is who He said He was; He is the Son of God, the Second Person of the Holy Trinity. He performed miracles none could explain, and no one else could do.

He said things no one else would say. He fulfilled all of the Old Testament prophecies regarding the Messiah, even though the prophecies were given hundreds of years apart and were beyond His control (i.e., a virgin birth, the city of His birth, His family tree, etc.). He prophesied His own death and

He had people willing to leave their homes, families, occupations, etc., to travel to the ends of the earth and eventually be martyred to carry on His teachings.

Resurrection. He had people willing to leave their homes, families, occupations, etc., to travel to the ends of the earth and eventually be martyred to carry on His teachings.

Beyond these points listed here, one must look at the history, growth, and timelessness of Christianity. Age after age evil has risen to do away with Christianity and has failed each time. The Church has lost some battles but will ultimately win the war, just as Christ promised us (Matthew 16:18).

SUGGESTED READING:
CCC 241, 477, 1559
Peter Kreeft, *Fundamentals of the Faith*
C. S. Lewis, *Mere Christianity*

THE NATURE AND VOCATION OF MAN

WHAT DOES IT MEAN TO SAY THAT HUMANS WERE MADE IN THE "IMAGE AND LIKENESS" OF GOD?

IN BRIEF:

Unlike everything else God created, we are made in the image and likeness of God, which means that human beings are unique within creation. We, alone, are capable of things like self-awareness, contemplation, and reflection. Only human beings have been given free will (the ability to determine our own actions) and an intellect (the ability to know God in a personal way). Also, through our immortal souls, we are able to share in God's own eternal life. While everything else in creation was made for human beings, we were made directly for God — to know and love Him and to enter into communion with Him. All of these things make us unique and reveal what it means to be made in the image and likeness of God.

IN DEPTH:

In Genesis 1:27 we read that God made human beings in His own "image and likeness." Before we look at what these words mean, we must first realize that this is said only about human beings. Of course God made the sun, moon, trees, plants, and animals, but in Scripture, none of those things are said to be made in God's image and likeness. That is a privilege given to human beings alone. This means that humans are unique among all that God has made. Because we are made in the image and likeness of God, we are fundamentally different from everything else that God has made. So what is it that makes us so special?

First of all, when God made human beings, He gave them dominion over all creation. Now, for some people dominion might sound like unrestricted power and authority to do whatever they want with creation, but this is a complete misunderstanding of what God has given to us. Instead of complete dominance and control, this dominion should be understood as stewardship. Stewardship is governing and caring for creation in ways that serve our needs *and* give honor and glory to God, the Creator. The dominion that we are given over creation is not so much a privilege, but rather a responsibility. In exercising this dominion over creation, we image God by sharing in His own power and authority.

Another thing that sets us apart from the rest of creation is our free will and our intellect. God has given each of us the freedom to choose our own path and make our own decisions. We aren't programmed to act a certain way or make certain choices. Instead, we are able to decide for ourselves what we will or will not do. We make these decisions by the power of our intellect and our ability to reason. We aren't governed solely by instinct; we are able to consider various options, reflect upon the potential harm and benefit of those options, and then determine what we think is best. We are able to reflect upon the meaning of life, the nature of love, the challenge of suffering, and other such things. Ants and parrots don't contemplate these sorts of things. Only humans have been given this capacity for self-reflection on the joys and challenges of life, and the power to freely choose their own path in life based on their use of human reason.

So what is so special about free will and reason? Again, just as our dominion over creation is a share in God's own power and authority, so also our free will is a share in God's own freedom, and our intellect is a participation in the very wisdom of God. God made us to share in His own life by knowing Him (through the power of our intellect) and loving Him (through the power of our free will). We exist so that God can share with us His own goodness. While all of creation was made for us, we were uniquely made for God. Among all creation, only we are capable of entering into a personal relationship with our Creator by knowing and loving Him.

Another insight is found in these words from the first chapter of Genesis. In Genesis 1:27 it says that God made man in His image and likeness, but this is immediately followed by these words, "male and female He created them." Part of our likeness to God is found in the fact that we were made male and female. Although there are male and female animals, they do not have the ability to love and sacrifice for another. That is something that is unique to humans. Men and women were made for each other so that they can enter into a life-giving communion of love. And this union of man and woman is meant to be an image and foretaste of our eternal communion with God. We were made for relationship, which images the relationship and exchange of love found in the Trinity. God, Himself, is a communion of love, and we were made to share in that communion. By being made male and female, we recognize that we are people made for communion.

Finally, central to understanding our uniqueness as creatures made in the image and likeness of God is the fact that we are composed of both body and soul. What makes us human beings (and not merely animals) is the fact that we are a unique union of body and soul. We are both physical and spiritual beings, and because of this, we are able to share in God's own life in a way unlike anything else in creation. This soul is created directly by God at the moment of our conception; it lives on even after our body dies, and it will be reunited with the body at the resurrection of the dead. The fact that we have an immortal soul is key to understanding what it means to be made in the image and likeness of God. We are, by nature, meant to live forever. Only mankind is capable of such an amazing thing.

SUGGESTED READING:

CCC 355-368
Blessed John Paul II, *Theology of the Body*
Peter Kreeft, *Catholic Christianity*, Chapters III-IV

THINGS TO CONSIDER:

> "Of all visible creatures only man is 'able to know and love his Creator.' He is 'the only creature on earth that God has willed for its own sake,' and he alone is called to share, by knowledge and love, in God's own life. It was for this end that he was created, and this is the fundamental reason for his dignity" (CCC 356).

> The term "soul" refers to "the innermost aspect of man, that which is of greatest value in him, that by which he is most especially in God's image: 'soul' signifies the spiritual principle in man" (CCC 363).

WHY DID GOD MAKE US MALE AND FEMALE?

IN BRIEF:

God made us male and female to be a reflection of Himself. We all know that when a man and a woman come together as one, this loving union is capable of leading to new life. But did you know that this union mirrors the Trinity? It's an image and a sign of God, who is a union of love between the Father, Son, and Holy Spirit that leads to life. God, who gives Himself to us in love and invites us to offer ourselves to Him in faith, created human beings male and female so that we, too, could give ourselves to one another and receive each other as a gift. The differences between the sexes are no accident, they were established by God to be a reflection of His own identity and of the relationship that we are called to have with Him.

IN DEPTH:

In the first chapters of Genesis we read about God creating human beings. But did you know that there are actually two accounts of creation? The first account (in Genesis 1) tells us that God created everything over the course of six "days" and that human beings were created on the sixth and final day of creation (with God "resting" on the seventh day from the work He had done). It is in this first creation account that we are told that human beings are unique; they are made in the "image and likeness of God." But then it immediately goes on to say that "God created man in His image, in the divine image He created him; male and female He created them" (Genesis 1:27). So, it seems that in some way being male and female is related to being in God's image.

In the second account (in Genesis 2) we hear a different story. According to this account, God first created a garden and then made a man (Adam) and placed him in it. But what is interesting is that the Bible says that God saw that the man was alone and that this was not good for him. So God made different kinds of animals for the man, but none of these animals turned out to be a suitable partner for Adam. God put the man into a deep sleep, took one of his ribs, and formed it into a woman (Eve). When the man woke up he said, "this one at last, is bone of my bone and flesh of my flesh" (Genesis 2:23). After seeing Eve, Adam realized that she was truly the suitable partner that God had made for him. What is most interesting is the fact that God wanted to make a partner for the man and that being alone was not good for the man.

In both of these accounts we see that the creation of both man and woman (male and female) was a conscious part of God's design of humanity. But why? Well, it wasn't because God just wanted to have different versions of human beings to add variety to His creation. God made human beings male and female to teach us that we were made for communion. We were made with the ability to experience life-giving love with the opposite sex. Through coming together as one, the man and the woman are able to give themselves to each other in love and receive each other as a gift.

God has made us out of love and for love. In fact, it is only in giving and receiving love that we can ever truly discover who we are meant to be, and this gift of self is uniquely manifested in the relationship between men and women. Just by looking at how God created our bodies, we can see that men and women were made for unity and communion with each other.

But as we saw in Genesis 1, this union is a reflection of God Himself; in the coming together of man and woman, both God's identity and man's vocation are revealed. As we said before, human beings were made for communion. But the communion of persons that is meant to exist between a man and woman in Matrimony is a sign or image of God is in His very nature. Remember, God is a communion of love between the Father, Son, and Holy Spirit. In His very essence, God is a life-giving communion of love. But through His love and goodness, He invites us to share in this communion.

The relationship of life-giving love that can exist between a man and a woman is meant to be a sign that points us to the relationship we are called to have with God – eternal communion in the Trinity.

This is why the Church has always upheld the equal dignity of all human beings, male and female. All of us, whether men or women, are called to communion and are made to share in the life giving love of God. But being equal in dignity isn't the same as being identical. The fact of the matter is that men and women are different. But in their differences they complement each other and serve as helpers to one another. God creating us male and female is all part of His plan, so that by the two coming together as one, they might be a reflection of God Himself.

SUGGESTED READING:
CCC 369-373
Pope John Paul II, *The Theology of the Body*
Katrina Zeno, *The Body Reveals God*
Fulton Sheen, *Three to Get Married*

THINGS TO CONSIDER:

"Man and woman were made 'for each other' – not that God left them half-made and incomplete: He created them to be a communion of persons" (CCC 372).

"God inscribed in the humanity of man and woman the vocation, and thus the capacity and responsibility, of love and communion. Love is therefore the fundamental and innate vocation of every human being" (John Paul II, *Familiaris Consortio*, 11).

"Their bond of love becomes the image and the symbol of the covenant which unites God and His people" (John Paul II, *Familiaris Consortio*, 12).

"[God] created them to be a communion of persons, in which each can be 'helpmate' to the other, for they are equal as persons and complementary as masculine and feminine" (CCC 372).

WHAT IS THE PURPOSE OF LIFE?

IN BRIEF:

The purpose of life is to get to heaven. As St. Augustine said, "God has made us for Himself, and our hearts are restless until they rest in Him." We were made to share in the very life of God, in the love, truth, and goodness of the Trinity. Nothing in this world can give us true fulfillment; it is only through knowing and loving God that we will ever truly be happy.

IN DEPTH:

There comes a time when each of us has to step back and ask ourselves some important questions: What is the point of all this? Where did I come from and where am I going? Having the right answer to these questions is essential. If we fail to understand the purpose of our lives, everything else that we do will be off track. To understand this, let's look at an analogy. Let's say someone gave you a box, and in this box are all the pieces that you need to build a dresser. But suppose that after looking at all of these pieces, you become convinced that the parts in the box are supposed to be used to build a refrigerator. If you believe this to be the purpose of those parts, you will never accomplish what you are meant to accomplish. No matter how hard you try, you will inevitably fail to fulfill the purpose for which those parts were made. Our lives are no different; there is a specific purpose or goal for our lives. The technical way of making this same point is to say that our lives are ordered to a specific *end*. When something is made, it is made for some purpose and that purpose could also be called an "end." We are created for a specific end; our lives are ordered toward (directed to) a specific goal. If we are mistaken about what this end or goal is, we will inevitably be unfulfilled and frustrated. If we don't recognize the proper end for which we were made, we will never reach our full potential.

Consider, for example, a chair. A chair is created for the purpose of being sat in. The chair is ordered to a specific end, namely, to be used for sitting. Now I could use the same chair as a baseball bat if I wanted to, but being a baseball bat is not its proper end, and so using it this way would be a disordered use of the chair (because it is not ordered to that end). Well, the same is true of our lives.

So what exactly is this end or goal that our lives are ordered? To understand the answer to this question we have to remember that God, in His very essence, is a communion of life, love, truth, and goodness. In this truth we discover the purpose of our lives. The very reason for our existence is to share in the inner life of the Trinity, to experience God's love in the most intimate way possible. We were made for heaven; we were made to see God "face to face" (1 Corinthians 13:12). This image of seeing God face to face is a way of saying that we were made to see God in His fullness, with nothing preventing us from seeing God as He truly is. The technical term for this is the *beatific vision*. This is the end to which we are ordered, to share in the very life of the Trinity in the glory of heaven. This is the reason for our existence and the meaning of our lives.

It is absolutely essential that we understand this; if we believe that anything less than the beatific vision is our purpose in life, we will never truly be happy. If we think that gaining popularity, money, fame, or pleasure is the ultimate goal of our lives, we will always be frustrated and empty inside. If we recognize God as the true purpose of our lives, everything else will be put in its proper place. When we understand that we are made for heaven, all other aspects of our lives will be seen in their proper perspective.

With this in mind, the answer to the question of why we are here becomes clear. We are here to know and love God and to work our way to heaven, where we will share in the joy of God's own life and love. As mentioned before, each of us has an end for which we were made. Our end is far greater than anything that can be found in this world; our end is the beatific vision, the knowledge of God as He truly is, a live-giving communion of love.

The purpose of life is to arrive at this end. How tragic it would be to seek our fulfillment in anything else and to settle for anything less than the glory of heaven. We were made for heaven, which means that our lives here on earth should be moving always in that direction. Knowing this changes everything. Once we know why we are here, this knowledge should affect everything: how we spend our time, what we choose to do and not do, and how we prioritize our lives. When we clearly see the purpose for our lives, the words of St. Paul become that much more important for us to take to heart: "Whatever is true, whatever is honorable, whatever is just, whatever is pure, whatever is lovely, whatever is gracious, if there is any excellence and if there is anything worthy of praise, think about these things" (Philippians 4:8).

SUGGESTED READING:

CCC 1023-1029
Viktor Frankl, *Man's Search for Meaning*
Frank Sheed, *A Map for Life*
St. Teresa of Avila, *Interior Castle*

THINGS TO CONSIDER:

"Because of His transcendence, God cannot be seen as He is, unless He, Himself, opens up His mystery to man's immediate contemplation and gives him the capacity for it. The Church calls this contemplation of God, in His heavenly glory, 'the beatific vision" (CCC 1028).

"God put us in the world to know, to love, and to serve Him, and so to come to paradise. Beatitude makes us 'partakers of the divine nature' and of eternal life. With beatitude, man enters into the glory of Christ and into the joy of the Trinitarian life" (CCC 1721).

WHAT IS GRACE AND WHY DO WE NEED IT?

IN BRIEF:

Grace is the gift of divine life and the help that God gives us to know and experience that life. It is like electricity, which provides the power needed for things to work. All of us are called to know and love God and to experience the very life and communion of the Trinity. But we can't accomplish this on our own; we are dependent upon God's help. Through grace, God provides the help and power that we need. Without it, we are like a coffee machine trying to make coffee without being plugged in. No matter how hard we try, we can't do it unless we are *connected to the power source.*

IN DEPTH:

Grace is one of those things that we might hear people talk about, but we may be really unclear about what grace actually is. When someone does something unexpected or difficult you might hear him or her say that they did it "by the grace of God." Or maybe you have sat in Mass on some Sunday and heard the priest speak about the grace that God wants to give us through the sacraments. Or you may be from a family that "says grace" before they eat. But what exactly is grace? Well, let's see what we come up with if we just go off of the situations mentioned above. We might say, okay, grace is some way of God helping us, something that He gives us, and something we have to be aware of (or "say") before we enjoy our favorite meal. Is that it? In some ways, this does give us a bit of a glimpse into what grace is. It is something that is given to us, something that helps and enables us to do things, and something that we must constantly be aware of in our daily lives. But let's see if we can break it open a bit further.

The first and most important point to keep in mind when we talk about grace is that we are called to a supernatural end ("end" here means "purpose" or "reason for existing" - for more on this, check out "What is the purpose of life? on page 38). There is a reason why we were made; there is a purpose for our lives. This purpose is not found in anything here on earth, but only in the life of God. (Which is why our end or purpose is "supernatural." It is beyond anything found in the natural world, the world we see and touch here on earth.) God is love. In His very essence, God is a communion of love and goodness between the Father, the Son, and the Holy Spirit. But God, in His love, offers us an invitation to share in that same inner life of love and goodness. This is why we are here. Our purpose is to enter into the very life of the Trinity. This is our reason for existing, to know and experience the love of God.

So what does this have to do with grace? Everything! Why? Because we cannot do this by our own ability. We need grace in order to meet our purpose. There is nothing within us (naturally) that would make us capable of entering into the very life and love of the Trinity. While it is true that we have a natural desire for God, this desire for God cannot be satisfied by our own effort alone. There is nothing that we can do on our own to raise ourselves up to share in God's own divine life. To reach this goal we must be elevated (or given special power) through grace. The purpose of our lives is to do something that we cannot do on our own ability, and this makes us completely dependent upon God's grace to help us.

Okay, so we know that we need grace, but what exactly is it? Simply put, grace is the free gift that God gives us to empower us to do what we were meant to do. Grace assists us and enables us to repent, have faith, and live according to the demands of the Gospel. This grace comes at the beginning of all of our good acts and brings them to their proper completion; there is never a time when we are not assisted, in some way, by God's grace to do what God calls us to do.

Now this "grace" that God gives us is described as either *sanctifying grace* or *actual grace*. Let's take a look at the different types of grace:

- Sanctifying grace is the grace that gives us a share in God's own life, making us pleasing to Him by being born again in new life as His children. Sanctifying grace actually changes us from the inside; it makes us holy and pleasing to God because it fills us with the very life of God.

- Actual grace is the particular help that God gives us to be faithful to Him in all of our decisions and behavior. It is the special power and assistance that God gives us to do good remain faithful, resist temptation, and repent when we sin.

Sanctifying grace makes us a part of the family of God; actual grace assists and empowers us to live in the way that being a part of His family requires. What is important to understand is that actual grace is there to help us at all stages of the game, from our initial conversion to our continuing faithfulness. We are dependent upon God's grace to accomplish what we are unable to do on our own. This is why grace is so essential. We need God's grace because we can't do it on our own. But God's love is so great that He not only calls us to share in His own life, but He also gives us all that we need to accomplish this supernatural purpose of our lives. This is why we say that all the good that we do or have is "by the grace of God;" this is why the sacraments are so important (as the way in which God continues to sustain our supernatural lives); and this is why we "say grace" before meals. We recognize that all that we have received is a gift.

All that we are, from our very existence to our relationship with God, has been accomplished by the free gift from God who desires for us to know and love Him, and that grace helps us do just that.

SUGGESTED READING:

CCC 1996-2016
Alan Schreck, *The Essential Catholic Catechism*, Chapter VIII
Fr. Matthias Scheeben, *The Glories of Divine Grace*

THINGS TO CONSIDER:

> *"Man is called to an end by nature that he cannot attain by nature, but only by grace because of the exalted character of the end"* (Thomas Aquinas, In Boeth. De Trinitate, 6,4, ad 5).

> Grace is the *"free and undeserved gift that God gives us to respond to His call to become children of God, adoptive sons, partakers of the divine nature and of eternal life"* (CCC 1996).

> "The grace of Christ is the gratuitous gift that God makes to us of His own life, infused by the Holy Spirit into our soul to heal it of sin and to sanctify it [...] Sanctifying grace is a habitual gift, a stable and supernatural disposition that perfects the soul itself to enable it to live with God, to act by His love" (CCC 1999-2000)

> "As actual grace, God gives us the help to conform our lives to His will" (CCC, Glossary).

WHAT IS TRUTH?

IS THERE SUCH A THING AS ABSOLUTE TRUTH?

IN BRIEF:

The irony of those who would say that there is no such thing as absolute truth is that, in saying this, they are using an absolute, universal claim to deny that there are any absolute, universal truths. They are saying that it is true, at all times and in all circumstances. However, at the same time, they are saying that there is nothing that could be true at all times and in all circumstances. Do you see a contradiction here?

But let's imagine that there is, in fact, no such thing as absolute truth. Now, if there is no standard by which our beliefs and actions are to be judged, then we could never really say that something is right or wrong. We could never say that one thing is true and the other false. But with this sort of relativism, if we were to really be consistent, we would have to be willing to accept that all beliefs are acceptable and valid if they were genuinely held to be true by others. This would be true even of those things that we personally think are wrong.

For example, if there were no absolute moral standards in life, we would have to be willing to say things like, "Well, I personally would never own a slave, but I can't really say that it is wrong for you to do so." If there were no absolute standards of morality, we might be able to argue over what is better or worse, but we could never really say, definitively, that things like slavery are wrong. This leads to an unacceptable relativism, which makes us the sole judges of what is right and good. This mentality is embodied in the often repeated phrase: "That might be true for you, but it's not true for me." This might be the case with some things (such as who we think the best football team is or the best guitarist is), but it can't be the case for everything, especially when it comes to morality. Some things just are, by their very nature, right and other things wrong; some things are true at all times and in all circumstances. The view that truth is whatever we want it to be is incompatible with the Catholic faith, which teaches that God is Truth and that our lives must be lived in conformity to the Truth.

IN DEPTH:

You know, on one level it would be awfully convenient if there were no such thing as absolute truth. If there was no final say as to what is true and what is false, you could never really be wrong, could you? I mean, if you were to have a discussion with someone and you were to come to what seemed like a real crossroad between what you think is true and what the other person thinks is true, you could always say: "Well, I guess we'll have to agree to disagree; your truth works for you and my truth works for me." Everyone goes away happy. No one has had to change their mind or admit that they might actually be wrong. Everyone gets to believe whatever they want. Sounds good, right?

The problem is that it just doesn't work that way. If there really is no absolute standard for truth, no final ground from which all things can be judged, anything goes. This really is not as good as it may initially sound, especially when it comes to morality. In fact, even people who say that they believe that morality is relative (meaning, it is determined by their own view and perspective) don't really believe this when it comes down to it.

Let's look at an example to see why absolute truth actually matters:

If someone decided that they wanted to kidnap you and make you their personal slave, what would you say? Most likely you would say that they couldn't do that and that it's just flat out wrong to enslave someone, but why would you say that? That may be what you think, but according to the other person's view of things, slavery may be just fine. If you were to say that they couldn't do this because slavery is wrong, you would be acknowledging that there are some things that are true in every time and place (which is what absolute truths are). In making your case you would most likely say that it doesn't matter that the person who kidnapped you personally thinks that slavery is morally acceptable; the fact of the matter is that it simply is not okay.

But why? Well, you could probably say that people should not be treated as mere objects to be used any way that someone wishes. But again, who is to say that this belief of yours is correct? It may work for you, but how can you say that the opposite view might not work for someone else? It may be "true for you" that people should not be treated as objects, but does this mean that it is true for everyone? What if someone genuinely believes that some people should be treated as objects and enslaved?

Well, let's imagine that the person who believes slavery to be right for them is then kidnapped and enslaved by someone else. If they were to really be consistent with their view on slavery, he or she would have to accept their situation without complaining. They would have to say, "Well, I can't really say that it is wrong to enslave me because that would be a violation of their view of what is right and wrong."

This is just absurd. Even a moral relativist wouldn't say that anything goes when it comes to morality. There have to be some guidelines that tell us what you should and should not do, but to present these guidelines they would probably say something like this: even though there is no absolute truth, someone can't do things that directly harm another person. But then the same question arises: what makes this principle (that a person should not cause direct harm to others) true? That principle might work for you, but how can you say that it is true for everyone?

Well, they might say that it is because human beings have a certain value or dignity that slavery violates. But wait a minute. All human beings? Doesn't this suggest that this universal dignity is somehow true at all times, in all places? This, again, is another absolute truth. If it were not absolute, we would have to accept that for someone else, the idea that some people are more valuable or worthy of respect might be true for them. If we are unwilling to accept this, we are left once again with holding to at least one absolute truth.

The fact of the matter is that saying that all truths are relative, that it is our own perspective that determines what is true and false or right and wrong, simply makes no sense. If you think of it on a much more basic level we can see that this is the case. Take, for example, the claim "God exists." Let's say that your friend Billy Bob denies this claim, and that you accept it. Can both be true? Is it really possible to say that God both does and does not exist? While you and Billy Bob may be free to hold different views on this, when it comes right down to it both views can't actually be true, can they? Either God exists or He doesn't. The same goes with some of the other basic claims of life. Either all people have an inherent dignity, or they don't. Either life is valuable and should be protected, or it is not and can be treated any way we wish. These claims can't all be true.

And yet, this is exactly how most people live, at least in practice. We like to think that what works for you is fine, and what works for me is fine. As long as no one is getting hurt, everyone is free to believe anything they want. Now, while it is true that we are free to believe whatever we want, does it really make sense to say that none of these beliefs are more or less true than others? Can it really be "true" that there is no absolute truth? To believe that there is no such thing as absolute truth leads us ultimately to anarchy, to accepting all ideas and all values as equally valid. This relativism is one of the fundamental problems of our world today. We must remember that we were made to know and embrace the truth. All discussions, investigations, and questions are meant to lead us forward to a deeper understanding of the truth. But if there is no truth, what are we journeying toward? If there is no truth to be obtained, then we are all just wasting our time.

As people of faith, we believe that God is truth, and that He has stamped this truth and the desire for it on the human heart. It is only through seeking the truth that we will truly be set free. While it is certainly valuable to engage in discussion and dialogue with others who have different beliefs and values, it is only when this is done with the goal of seeking to grow closer to what is, in fact, true that these discussions can actually be fruitful. If both nothing and anything is true, we are left as the creators of our own reality. But, there is only one reality, and our views of the world must be judged according to whether or not they are in line with this reality. This, and only this, is what determines the truth or our beliefs.

SUGGESTED READING:

CCC 215-217, 2464-2492
Peter Kreeft, *The Refutation of Moral Relativism*
G. K. Chesterton, *Orthodoxy*
Benjamin Wiker, *10 Books that Screwed Up the World*
Peter Kreeft, *How to Win a Culture War*

THINGS TO CONSIDER:

"We are moving towards a dictatorship of relativism which does not recognize anything as certain and which has as its highest goal one's own ego and one's own desires" (Pope Benedict XVI).

"Man tends by nature toward the truth. He is obliged to honor and bear witness to it: 'It is in accordance with their dignity that all men, because they are persons [...] are both impelled by their nature and bound by a moral obligation to seek the truth, especially religious truth. They are also bound to adhere to the truth once they come to know it and direct their whole lives in accordance with the demands of truth'" (CCC 2467).

"Truth is the agreement or conformity of reality and the mind's judgment on reality. It is 'the equation of thought to thing'" (Msgr. Paul J. Glenn, A Tour of the Summa, 19).

WHAT IS NATURAL LAW?

IN BRIEF:

The natural law is the standard of truth and morality that binds all people, in all times and places. It is discovered by the use of our human reason and must always conform to the eternal truth of God and the way that He has created the world to be. We are not free to determine for ourselves what is right and true. Instead, we are subject to the truth of reality that God has established. Through following the standards of the natural law, we seek to conform our lives to God, who is truth and goodness itself.

IN DEPTH:

The concept of the "natural law" can be difficult to understand. Basically, the natural law refers to those moral truths that are written (in the language of the Bible) upon our hearts (take a look at Romans 2:12-16). It is called "natural" because it is, in a certain sense, written into our very nature. Since God (who is truth) made us, He has embedded within us a standard of truth and morality that is a reflection of Himself. Philosophers and theologians have determined that there are *four types* of laws. It's important to understand these different types of laws before going further into what natural law is.

The first type of law is the *eternal law*. The eternal law is essentially the truth of reality in the mind of God. This phrase "in the mind of God" is a strange term for many people, but it can be understood this way: God is truth, and He has created and established all things in accordance with the truth; the eternal law refers to how God *knows the world to be*. Now, obviously, God made the world the way it is, but since God is truth itself, the truth of reality finds its ultimate source in God Himself. The eternal law is the ultimate basis of every other law because it is the source and standard of truth itself. God created the world with a certain order, and He knows this order perfectly because He, Himself, is the source of it. This is what we call the eternal law in the mind of God.

The second type of law is the *natural law*, which is our sharing in the eternal law by the use of our human reason (more on this in a minute).

The third type of law is *revealed law*. This refers to those truths that God has specifically revealed to us for the sake of guiding us according to what is good and true. In the Old Testament God revealed His law (Torah) to the people of Israel in order to guide them in a right relationship with Him and one another. And in the New Testament, Jesus reveals the fullness of God's law in order to lead us toward our ultimate end (to know and love God and share in His divine life). There is a lot of overlap between revealed law and the natural law. Even though there are many truths that we are able to know by the use of human reason alone, our sin often blinds us from seeing this truth clearly. So, God chose to reveal some of those truths contained in the natural law so that all people might know these things with certainty. As St. Thomas Aquinas says, God has revealed even the truths that we can discover through human reason so that these truths might be known "by all men with ease, with firm certainty, and with no admixture of error" (*CCC* 38).

The fourth type of law is *civil law*. These are the laws that govern human beings and civil society. We create them for the purpose of benefiting the good of all mankind but their validity and binding force is dependent upon the degree to which they conform to the natural law. Just because something is considered "legal" in the eyes of the law doesn't necessarily mean that it is "moral." When civil laws do not conform to the natural law (such as in the case of abortion or racial discrimination being "legal") they are unjust or immoral laws and so should not be followed.

Now, back to the natural law. The natural law is our ability to use the gift of human reason and our intellect to discover the truth of reality and conform our lives to it. This law is called natural because reason, which is a fundamental part of human nature, is the way by which we are able to grasp these truths.

The natural law affirms that truth and goodness do, in fact, exist, and that through our use of human reason, we can discover these things. The natural law stands as the basis and foundation of moral law, which means that we judge morality according to the degree to which it conforms to the natural law. The precepts of the natural law are universal, binding upon all people in all times (which goes back to our last question about absolute truth).

All of this points to the fact that standards of morality are not something that we can determine for ourselves. We are not the creators of what is right and wrong; we are subject to the truth as

God has established it. We are subject to the eternal law, which is the way God knows the world to be. Because of this, we must seek to discover the truth of God rather than seek to create our own sense of truth.

SUGGESTED READING:

CCC 1950-1960
Peter Kreeft, *Fundamentals of the Faith*
Dale Ahlquist, *Common Sense 101: Lessons from G. K. Chesterton*

THINGS TO CONSIDER:

"God's truth is His wisdom, which commands the whole created order and governs the world" (CCC 216).

St. Thomas Aquinas makes this comparison: "A governor has in mind the type of order he desires among his subjects. God is the infinite and all-perfect governor. God therefore has in Himself the 'type' of what creatures are to do to attain their end and purpose. This 'type' is divine wisdom viewed as eternal law. Hence, we say, 'The eternal law is the type of divine wisdom directing all acts and movements'" (Msgr. Paul J. Glenn, A Tour of the Summa, 168).

"If rulers were to enact unjust laws or take measures contrary to the moral order, such arrangements would not be binding in conscience" (CCC 1903).

"The natural law expresses the original moral sense which enables man to discern by reason the good and the evil, the truth and the lie" (CCC 1954).

"In the diversity of cultures, the natural law remains as a rule that binds men among themselves and imposes on them, beyond the inevitable difference, common principles" (CCC 1957).

WHO DETERMINES WHAT IS RIGHT AND WRONG? WHAT MAKES SOMETHING MORALLY RIGHT?

IN BRIEF:

God's law is the ultimate standard for determining what is right and wrong. The way that we decide if particular actions are right or wrong is by looking at the object (the thing being done), the intention (our reason for doing it), and the circumstances (when and where) of the act. Only those acts whose object, intention, and circumstances are collectively understood to be good can be considered good or right actions. If any one of these three things is bad, the act as a whole is bad or immoral.

IN DEPTH:

This is a great question, and thankfully, our Church sets forth criteria for figuring this out. According to Catholic teaching, an action is morally right or good if the *object*, the *intention*, and the *circumstances* in which it is done are *all* good. If any one of these things (the object, intention, or circumstance) is not good, then the act itself is judged to be morally wrong. So let's take a look at these three things.

The *object* of an act refers to the thing that is being done. This can obviously be a number of things, from fasting or prayer to stealing or murder. Our actions involve doing some thing, and this thing that we are doing is the object of our action. The *intention* refers to the desired goal of our action, the reason for our doing the thing in the first place. Everything we do is done for some purpose, and this purpose is the intention of our act. The *circumstances* refer to the conditions in which our act takes place. It is the when, where, and how of our actions. In order for an action to be morally right or good, all three of these things must be good.

Let's take a look at an example to try and make sense of how this applies to individual acts. Consider fasting. Abstaining from certain foods or drinks as a spiritual exercise is certainly a good object. Now let's say that this is done on a day in which your are able to abstain without causing any harm or offense to yourself or someone else. (For example, fasting on a day in which someone is planning a birthday party for you or on a day that you are supposed to run a marathon may not be the best circumstances in which to fast). But now, let's say that your intention in fasting isn't to enter into greater prayerful union with God or for the sake of solidarity with those who unwillingly go hungry (both of which would be good intentions), but for the sake of appearing to be holy to others. This sort of self-serving intention would not be considered a good intention. And in this case, even though fasting (of itself) is good, the act as a whole will not be considered good because the bad intention has corrupted an otherwise good act.

Now, one thing that is important to realize is that some actions are always wrong by the very nature of their object. This means that there are some things that are *in and of themselves* morally wrong, independent of any intention or circumstance. The Church calls these things *intrinsic evils*. In the case of intrinsic evils there are no good intentions or circumstances that can change or undo the sinfulness of the bad object. For example, directly killing an innocent human being is, of its very nature, contrary to the moral law. There are no intentions and circumstances that can change this; it is simply intrinsically evil (morally unacceptable in every circumstance).

This three-fold way of determining the moral quality of an act is the standard by which we should judge our actions. But why is it so important that we always seek to do what is morally good? Someone might say that if we don't, we run the risk of going to hell. That is true, but we weren't made just to avoid hell; we were made to experience the fullness of life as God intended it. God wants what is truly best for us. When we sin (do moral evil), we actually harm our own and others' ability to realize our full potential.

God wants us to do what is right because by doing right, we establish the conditions necessary for all people to live according to the dignity that they possess. When we turn away from God's law, we prevent ourselves and others from living in a manner worthy of their dignity as children of God destined for eternal life. God calls us to holiness because that is truly what we were meant to be: holy. It is God who says what is right and wrong, and He determines what is right and wrong because He knows what will truly lead us to our goal: eternal life.

SUGGESTED READING:

CCC 1749-1756
Blessed John Paul II, *Memory and Identity*
Peter Kreeft, *Back to Virtue*

THINGS TO CONSIDER:

"The object of the choice can itself vitiate an act in its entirety. There are some concrete acts – such as fornication – that it is always wrong to choose, because choosing them entails a disorder of the will, that is, a moral evil" (CCC 1755).

"Everyone should look upon his neighbor (without any exception) as another self, bearing in mind above all his life and the means necessary for living it in a dignified way" (Gaudium et Spes, 27).

ARE FAITH AND REASON INCOMPATIBLE?

IN BRIEF:

Faith and reason are both given to us as a gift from God. Through reason we are able to discover many truths about God, ourselves, and the world around us. Through faith God reveals many of these same truths, as well as truths that go beyond human reason (such as God as a Trinity of persons). Faith and reason never truly contradict each other since both are concerned with the discovery of truth, of which God is the source and basis.

IN DEPTH:

This question is very closely related to another question: do science and religion contradict each other? Many people tend to say that we should really only listen to what science tells us and that religion contradicts science, and so it cannot be trusted. The problem is that this assumes that what science teaches and what religion teaches are actually opposed to each other, but that is just not the case.

Our society places a great deal of importance upon science and technology, and rightfully so. The scientific discoveries made over the years have been pretty incredible. But, science can never (and will never) contradict God. Why? Because science is the study of God's *creation*. Whether it's the solar system or human beings, scientists are seeking to understand the chemical and biological systems that God, in His power and wisdom, established.

The Church actually has great respect for human reason and science because they can lead to many truths and help explain God's creation. But it is foolish to try to pit science and religion against one another because it is impossible.

Science and religion (or reason and faith) are really just two different ways to come to know the same truths. Now, we must acknowledge that there are certain truths of faith that science and reason simply cannot know by themselves (such as the nature of Jesus as fully God and fully man, or that God, in His very essence, is a Trinity of three persons, Father, Son, and Holy Spirit). But there are other truths (such as the existence of God and precepts of the natural law) that can be known by both faith and reason. Through science and human reason we are able to look at the world around us and discover that there must be something (or someone) that caused everything to exist. Through faith, we are told that God created the heavens and the earth. The same truth is being affirmed here, but it is arrived at in two different ways: through reason we ascend to God's existence from what we see around us, and through faith God brings down to us, by revelation, the truth of His existence.

Now what about the so-called contradictions between faith and reason (or religion and science)? Well, as we said before, there can be no actual contradiction between these two. If there is, either the scientific teaching is wrong or the religious teaching is wrong. Many people like to look at the Book of Genesis, which says that God created the world in six days, to say that what we know about the world through science goes against this teaching of the Bible. The problem though is that these first chapters of Genesis were never intended to tell us *how* God created the world. They weren't meant to teach us scientific truths about the world but religious truths about God, about ourselves, and about our relationship with Him and all of creation.

However, there is a bigger issue here. It seems that most people who try to set faith and reason against each other are doing so because they want to discount the claims of religion so that they don't have to listen to what it says. It seems that if all we do is follow what science tells us, we are set free from a lot of moral constraints. For example, if you want to have an affair, listening only to science would be very convenient since science doesn't say anything about the morality of adultery. If you want to steal from your employer or stay home from Mass on Sundays, science doesn't have much to say here either. Now, I am not at all claiming that scientists are adulterous thieves who don't go to Mass. (Many scientists or philosophers are, in fact, faithful believers in God.) But what I am saying is that using science or human reason to try to discredit faith and religion can be quite convenient if you already have a desire to live in ways contrary to religion.

The fact of the matter is that human reason is one of the greatest gifts that God has given to us. Through it we are able to discover many truths about God, truths that are often confirmed and taught in religion as well. Since both science and religion are ultimately concerned with discovering truth, they actually complement one another. For there is only one truth, even if there are different ways of knowing this truth.

SUGGESTED READING:

CCC 153-159

Fr. Robert Spitzer, *New Proofs for the Existence of God: Contributions of Contemporary Physics and Philosophy*

Peter Kreeft and Ronald Tacelli, *Handbook of Christian Apologetics*

THINGS TO CONSIDER:

> *"Methodical research in all branches of knowledge, provided it is carried out in a truly scientific manner and does not override moral laws, can never conflict with the faith, because the things of the world and the things of faith derive from the same God"* (CCC 159).

> *"There can never be any real discrepancy between faith and reason. Since the same God who reveals mysteries and infuses faith has bestowed the light of reason on the human mind, God cannot deny Himself, nor can truth ever contradict truth"* (CCC 159).

THE NEED
FOR AUTHORITY

WHO CAN INTERPRET THE BIBLE? (THE DILEMMA)

IN BRIEF:

When we discuss the Bible with others, especially when we come across disagreements about what it means, people usually want to jump right in and start throwing verses at each other to prove their point. But before we do this, it's important to look at a dilemma that must be addressed before really entering into the discussion.

IN DEPTH:

Have you ever come across Scripture verses that seem to have different possible interpretations, such as Jesus' words at the Last Supper, "This is my body" (Matthew 26:26)? Or verses that seem to contradict each other, such as "a person is justified by faith apart from works of the law," (Romans 3:28) and "a person is justified by works and not by faith alone" (James 2:24)?

These examples show us that the Bible is not always self-explanatory, and that some passages require a choice of one interpretation over another. But these choices have resulted in disagreements between sincere, committed Christians about exactly what the Bible teaches.

These examples show us that the Bible is not always self-explanatory, and that some passages require a *choice* of one interpretation over another. But these choices have resulted in disagreements between sincere, committed Christians about exactly what the Bible teaches.

Now, let's say that we're to choose an interpretation of a certain verse that is different from another Christian's interpretation. How do you know which interpretation is the correct one?

Someone might want to say that they experience a certain peace and joy that comes from being in a right relationship with Christ, and so their interpretation must be correct. Well, what if you also experience this peace and joy in your life but have still come to a different interpretation? How do you know which interpretation is correct?

Now, someone might be tempted to say that we must "agree to disagree," but would this mean that we *can't* know for sure which person has arrived at the correct interpretation? Does the New Testament teach us that Jesus built a Church in which it would be impossible for His followers to know the truth about what to believe and how to live? Didn't Jesus say, "You will know the truth, and the truth will set you free" (John 8:32) and "When He comes, the Spirit of truth, He will guide you to all truth" (John 16:13)?

At this point, someone might respond by saying that their interpretation is the correct one because they have asked the Holy Spirit to guide them as they read the Bible. But what if you have done the same thing, and yet you still arrive at different interpretations?

We, the readers of the Bible, cannot be the final authority regarding its interpretation, otherwise, we will always be faced with the question, "How do you know that your interpretation is correct?"

Well, they could say that they are accepting their interpretation "on faith," but in what are they placing their faith? If both of you are trusting in God to lead you to the correct interpretation, but you still disagree, does this mean that God is leading people in different directions? *If God were in fact leading all sincere, committed Christians in their interpretation of the Bible, would they arrive at different conclusions?* It doesn't seem so. But if He is not leading *all* Christians to the correct interpretation, but only some, how do you know for sure that He is leading you?

Well, some might say that Christians only disagree on smaller, less important matters. But how do we know what is and is not important? Who decides this importance? If you and I decide, how do we know that our decision is not mistaken?

Do you see the dilemma? We, the readers of the Bible, cannot be the final authority regarding its interpretation, otherwise, we will always be faced with the question, "How do you know that your interpretation is correct?" If there is no way out of this dilemma, then it is pointless to even discuss the meaning of the

Bible because our arguments will always be nothing more than "opinion" and "personal interpretation." Herein lies the dilemma.

The authority of our interpretation must come from some source that is free from error, from someone or something that we can absolutely trust to correctly interpret the Bible.

So, is there a way out of this dilemma? Yes! The authority of our interpretation must come from some source that is free from error, from someone or something that we can absolutely trust to correctly interpret the Bible. This person is Christ, the Son of God who has been raised from the dead, and this thing is the Catholic Church, which Christ set up and to which He gave authority to teach in His name. This role of the Church as the interpreter of the Bible will be discussed in more detail in the following questions.

SUGGESTED READING:
Mark Shea, *Making Sense Out of Scripture*
Dave Armstrong, *The Catholic Verses*

WHAT IS THE RULE OF FAITH?

IN BRIEF:

The "Rule of Faith" refers to a standard that is used to judge whether or not a particular idea or teaching is consistent with the truth that Jesus revealed. It is a sort of measuring stick that is used to determine what is and what is not true Christian teaching. The standard that the Catholic Church uses is apostolic teaching. It is the message and preaching of the apostles and the bishops that followed that the Church uses to judge the true understanding of all that Jesus said and did.

IN DEPTH:

This is probably a phrase that you haven't come across before, so let's first explain what we mean by "Rule of Faith" before we go on to answer the question.

For most of us, the word "rule" probably makes us think of some law or policy that we have to follow, but this isn't what we are talking about in this case. What we mean by "rule" is a standard that is used to measure, judge, or test something. For example, if you want to know if a basketball hoop is regulation height, you would use a measuring tape to test the height of the rim and see if it measures up to the standard ten feet. In this case the measuring tape would be the standard (or rule) by which you would decide whether the hoop is regulation height.

Now, if we keep this understanding of "rule" in mind, how should the phrase "Rule of Faith" be understood? Well, if a rule is a standard used to judge or measure something, then the Rule of Faith would be some standard that is used to judge or measure the Catholic faith. But what do we mean here by "faith"? Although we normally think of faith as our trust in God and our obedience to Him (which is a correct way to understand faith), in this case we mean something a little different. What we are talking about is the *truth* that God has revealed to us for our salvation, we are talking about *divine revelation*.

Divine revelation is all that God has told us about who He is and how we are supposed to live in relationship with Him and each other. So when we talk about "faith" we are talking about all that

God has taught. The "Rule of Faith" is some thing or standard (rule) that is used to judge Christian truth (the faith). The "Rule of Faith" is a standard used to judge whether or not something is in line with divine revelation (the truth that we have received from God).

You might be asking yourself, "Why is it necessary to have a Rule of Faith in the first place?"

Well, if someone were to make some claim about Jesus (let's say, that He was not the Son of God), how would you determine whether or not the statement was consistent with Christian teaching? Anyone can make any claim they want about Jesus, but this does not mean that all of these statements are true.

Part of what makes Christianity *Christianity* is the fact that it accepts only what is true about who Jesus is. Not all statements about Jesus measure up to the truth about Jesus that forms the basis of the Christian faith. So how do we determine whether or not claims about Jesus are consistent with the truth that Christ revealed? One way to determine this is by going to the Bible (specifically to one of the Gospels) and judging statements about Jesus by the standard of the words of the Bible. In this case, the "Rule of Faith" (or standard of judgment) would be the Bible. Now there is nothing wrong with turning to the Bible as a standard of Christian teaching. But what about before the Bible was written? What would have been the Rule of Faith then?

Now, it is important to realize that the New Testament was not written until long after Christianity had begun and began to spread. (In fact the books of the New Testament were not officially put together in a collection until the fourth century, nearly four hundred years after Christ.) So, how did the first Christians learn the faith?

The answer is that it was through the teaching of the apostles that Christians first learned the saving truth that God had revealed through Christ. Remember, it was the apostles who were given the mission to preach the Gospel to the entire world:

> *"Jesus approached and said to them, 'All authority in heaven and on earth has been given to me. Go, therefore, and make disciples of all nations, baptizing them in the name of the Father, and of the Son, and of the Holy Spirit, teaching them to observe all that I have commanded you'" (Matthew 28:18-20).*

This means that the Gospel was being preached and taught before the individual Gospels were ever written; and when someone made a claim about Jesus in the early Church, the truth of that claim was judged and measured according to whether or not it was consistent with the teaching of the apostles. While it might seem natural to turn to the Bible as the "Rule of Faith," in the early Church this just wasn't an option. For them the standard used to judge the true Christian faith was apostolic teaching. The apostles were given the task and authority to preach the true message of Christ, and it was the teaching of these apostles that formed the standard (or rule) of the Christian faith.

The authority of the apostles to authentically interpret and pass on the true teaching of Christ then passed on to those who continued to lead the Church after the apostles were gone. These people (the bishops of the early Church were called the "successors" of the apostles) had the power and responsibility to teach the Christian faith in the name of Christ and the apostles; it was the teaching of these bishops that continued to be the "Rule of Faith," the standard by which the true message of Christ was judged.

So then what is the "Rule of Faith"? It is apostolic teaching: the teaching of the apostles and the successors appointed by them to pass on the Faith to every generation. And where is apostolic teaching found today? Well, this will be discussed more fully in the next two sections, but the brief answer is that this teaching is contained in both Sacred Scripture (the Bible) and Sacred Tradition (the teaching of the apostles passed down through the bishops), and it is interpreted by the Magisterium (the authoritative teachings of the Pope and Bishops of the Church). If these terms are new to you, don't worry. Keep reading; Scripture, Tradition, the Magisterium, and the way they are related to each other will be discussed in more detail.

SUGGESTED READING:
Dei Verbum
CCC 74-100
Pope Benedict XVI, *Jesus of Nazareth*
Scott Hahn, *Reasons to Believe*

THINGS TO CONSIDER:

> "It pleased God, in His goodness and wisdom, to reveal Himself and to make known the mystery of His will... The most intimate truth which this revelation gives us about God and the salvation of man shines forth in Christ, who is Himself both the mediator and the sum total of Revelation" (Dei Verbum, 2).

> "Take as your norm the sound words that you heard from me" (2 Timothy 1:13).

> "As we have said before, and now I say again, if anyone preaches to you a Gospel other than the one that you received, let that one be accursed" (Galatians 1:9).

> "What you heard from me through many witnesses entrust to faithful people who will have the ability to teach others as well" (2 Timothy 2:2).

WHICH CAME FIRST: THE BIBLE OR THE CHURCH?

IN BRIEF:

Jesus didn't come down from heaven with the Bible in His hands. Nor did He spend His 33 years on earth writing a New York Times best seller. Surprisingly enough, He didn't even tell His followers to write anything down. Instead, He chose to gather people around Himself, to teach them about the Kingdom of God, and to form them into a community founded upon Peter and the apostles. He formed a community that we now call the Church. This Church began when the Holy Spirit came down upon the apostles, and they began to preach the Gospel and invite people to follow Christ and be baptized. It was not until later that the writings of the New Testament (and eventually the Bible as a whole) were produced *by the Church*. All of this means that it is the Church, not the Bible, that came first.

IN DEPTH:

Have you ever thought about this? For most of us who have grown up in any sort of Christian family or tradition, we probably have never considered a time without the Bible. We can go to any store and buy a variety of translations of the Bible at any time. We can even find the Bible on the Internet with just a few clicks of the mouse. There is a pretty good chance that most of us take the Bible for granted.

However, if we stop and think about it, we realize that this is obviously not the case. We know, for example, that Jesus did not come with a Bible in hand to give to His followers. He did have the Old Testament (which, by the way, wouldn't have been called the "Old" Testament in Jesus' time, it was simply referred to as "the Scriptures"), but even the earliest parts of the New Testament were not written until at least 30 years after Jesus' death and Resurrection. We also have to remember that the New Testament wasn't written down in one sitting by one person. The New Testament is a collection of different writings, and it was written by different people, at different times and places, and to different audiences. These individual writings were not put together in a collection until much later. So, while this might seem strange in an age where everything is reported and documented as it happens, we have to realize that the Gospel writers did not write down Jesus' words and actions as they were happening.

Why does this matter? Because many people want to turn to the Bible as the sole basis of Christian teaching. For a lot of people, the Bible is the bottom line when it comes to what is true and what is false. But this could only work if the Bible came before the Church. The idea falls apart if the Church came before the Bible. So which is it? Well, first of all, we know that Jesus came to build a Church. He told Simon Peter, "You are Peter, and upon this rock I will build my church" (Matthew 16:18). Jesus makes it clear that He is building a Church, and this Church will be built upon the foundation of Simon Peter and the rest of the apostles. They are the ones that were given the unique task of spreading the Gospel and making disciples of all the nations (Matthew 28:19).

So, Jesus came to build a Church, and this Church was founded upon the apostles and their work of spreading the Gospel. But when did this all start? When did the apostles begin this great mission? We find the answer in the Acts of the Apostles. After Jesus' Resurrection and Ascension, the apostles received the gift of the Holy Spirit that Jesus promised would be sent after He returned to the Father. Scripture tells us that the apostles "were all in one place together. And suddenly there came from the sky a noise like a strong driving wind, and it filled the entire house in which they were. Then there appeared to them tongues as of fire, which parted and came to rest on each one of them. And they were all filled with the Holy Spirit and began speaking in different tongues, as the Spirit enabled them to proclaim" (Acts 2:1-4). There they were, gathered together in a room when all of the sudden a wind came blowing through, and they saw "tongues as of fire" descend upon them. What these tongues of fire actually looked like, we don't really know. But what we do know is that through this they were filled with the Holy Spirit and began to speak in different languages (that is what speaking in "different tongues" means here). Now, what is most interesting is what happens next.

Peter began to preach and proclaim the Gospel. He began a long speech about how God sent His own Son into the world to save it from sin. Even though He was rejected and put to death, He rose from the dead and brought new life to those who followed Him. This is an important event. It is the first time that Jesus' command to the apostles (to make disciples of all nations) was carried out. As a result, about 3000 people accepted Peter's message and were baptized. Through the coming of the Holy Spirit, the Church was born, and through the preaching of the apostles, the community of believers began to grow.

This was only months after Jesus' death and Resurrection, before any part of the New Testament was ever written. This means that the Church was alive and growing before the Bible, as we know it, was put together. It is important to see that the answer to our original question is that it was the Church that came first, not the Bible. The apostles were proclaiming the Gospel before any of the individual Gospels were ever written. The Christian community was growing and praying together before any of the New Testament letters (or epistles) were ever written by St. Paul. In fact, all of the individual books of the New Testament were actually produced, written, and passed around from within the Church. And it was the Church (specifically Catholic bishops) who had to decide, over hundreds of years, which, books should and should not be a part of the New Testament.

So, why does any of this matter? Well it all goes back to the last question on the Rule of Faith. The standard used to judge what was true to Jesus' message in the early Church was not the Bible (it couldn't have been, it wasn't around yet), but rather apostolic teaching. And this teaching was found in the Church, specifically in the teaching of the popes and bishops appointed by Peter and the apostles to continue the mission entrusted to them. This is why St. Paul tells St. Timothy that the Church is "the pillar and foundation of truth" (1 Timothy 3:15). It is the Church — those who follow Christ under the leadership of those commanded to guard and proclaim the Gospel (the pope and the bishops) — that guarantees the truth of the Bible. As St. Augustine said, "I would not believe in the Gospels were it not for the authority of the Catholic Church" (*Against the Letter of Mani Called "The Foundation"* 5:6).

It is only because the Church is guided by the Holy Spirit and has a share in the authority of Jesus Christ that we even have the Bible in the first place. All of this will be looked at in more detail in the next two sections, but for now, we must realize that it was the Church that came first, not the Bible.

SUGGESTED READING:

CCC 120-133
Alan Schreck, *The Compact History of the Catholic Church*
Scott Hahn, *Spirit & Life*

THINGS TO CONSIDER:

Ascension: "The entry of Jesus' humanity into divine glory in God's heavenly domain, forty days after His Resurrection" (CCC Glossary).

"He enjoined them not to depart from Jerusalem, but to wait for 'the promise of the Father about which you have heard me speak'" (Acts 1:4). "The Advocate, the Holy Spirit that the Father will send in my name, He will teaching you everything and remind you of all that I told you" (John 14:26).

The word "gospel" literally means good news. What is this Good News? That God's mercy and love have been fully revealed in the life, death, and Resurrection of Jesus Christ.

IS THE CATHOLIC CHURCH A "BIBLE CHURCH"?

IN BRIEF:

What most people mean by "Bible church" is a church that looks to the Bible alone as the sole basis of Christian teaching. In this case, the Catholic Church is not a "Bible church." It is an apostolic Church. Why? The only way the Catholic Church could be considered a "Bible church" is if Jesus came down from heaven with a Bible in hand and spent His entire life making copies of it and spreading it around. But it just didn't happen that way. Instead, He chose twelve men (the apostles), to whom He entrusted His message, and He gave them authority to teach in His name. It wasn't until much later that the Bible, as we know it, came around as a product of the Church, not the basis of it. For this reason, the Catholic Church cannot be considered a "Bible church."

IN DEPTH:

You may not have heard this phrase before, but when most people speak of a "Bible church" what they usually mean is a church that looks to the Bible, and only the Bible, in figuring out what to believe. The idea here is that the Bible is the only source of truth when it comes to the Christian faith, and so any Church, if it's going to be true to what Jesus taught, must teach only those things that are taught in the Bible. This all sounds good enough, right? It seems obvious that we would want to belong to a Church whose beliefs are found in and based upon what is taught in the Bible. So, this brings us to our original question, is the Catholic Church a "Bible church"?

There are some people (in fact, you may be one of them) who would accuse the Catholic Church of not being a Bible church. They would say that Catholics believe things that are not found in the Bible, or worse, things that go directly against what is taught in the Bible. They would say that things like Purgatory or Confession are not found in the Bible, and so the Catholic Church cannot be considered a Bible church, since it teaches things (supposedly) not taught in the Bible. Now, we aren't going to look at these specific topics here. (Don't worry. We will later so keep reading.) But what is our response to this accusation? Is the Catholic Church a "Bible church" or not?

This may surprise you, but the Catholic Church is not a "Bible church." Why not? Well, it's not because Catholic beliefs are not found in or based upon the Bible; they definitely are. It's also not because the Church teaches things that go against the teachings of the Bible; it doesn't. The Catholic Church is not a "Bible church" because it does not accept the idea that the Bible *alone* is the sole source of Christian truth. This idea will be discussed in more detail later (see the question: "What is Tradition, and how does it relate to the Bible?" on page 84) but for now it is important to realize that if we define a "Bible church" as a church that looks to the Bible and only the Bible as the source of truth, the Catholic Church cannot be considered a "Bible church." This isn't a criticism of the Church because the Catholic Church was never meant to be a "Bible church."

Jesus set up His Church to be an apostolic Church, one that is built upon the teaching and witness of those twelve men who were sent by Jesus into the world to spread the good news of the Gospel. If Jesus wanted His Church to be a "Bible church," He would have spent His 33 years on earth writing a really good book and then given it to His followers with the command to go make copies and give it to everyone they met. But He didn't do this. Why? Because Christianity isn't about a book; it's about a relationship. Jesus didn't come just to give us wise teachings or directions on how to live good moral lives (although this is certainly an important part of the Gospel). No, He came to give us much more than that; He came to invite us into a relationship of love and life with the blessed Trinity. This is the heart of Jesus' message: Come, follow me, and I will lead you home.

But how was this message spread? It wasn't through a book, though some of it eventually was written down. Rather, it was through those twelve men, who had known Jesus most intimately, that the good news of salvation and the invitation to new life was spread.

> *"He commissioned us to preach to the people and testify that He is the one appointed by God as judge of the living and the dead. To Him all the prophets bear witness, that everyone who believes in Him will receive forgiveness of sins through His name."*
> - Acts 10:42-43

This is why we profess our belief not in a "Bible church" but in one, holy, catholic, and *apostolic* Church.

Although some of this message eventually was written down and collected into the Bible as we now know it, it was the apostles and those that followed who were given the authority to guard, interpret, and pass on Christ's message. For this reason, the Catholic Church is an apostolic Church, not a "Bible church."

SUGGESTED READING:
Dei Verbum
CCC 50-141
Dave Armstrong, *The Catholic Verses*
John Bergsma, *Bible Basics for Catholics*

THINGS TO CONSIDER:

> The Second Vatican Council taught that "the Church does not draw her certainty about all revealed truths from the holy Scriptures alone [...] both Scripture and Tradition must be accepted and honored with equal feelings of devotion and reverence" (Dei Verbum, 9).

> "The Christian faith is not a 'religion of the book.' Christianity is a religion of the 'Word' of God, a word which is 'not a written and mute word, but the Word which is incarnate and living'" (CCC 108).

THE BIBLE

HOW CAN I BE SURE THE BIBLE REALLY IS THE WORD OF GOD AND IS RELIABLE?

IN BRIEF:

Countless people try to say that the Bible is "unreliable" or "outdated." Many people – some of whom are well-read and quite intellectual – do everything they can to debunk the validity of Scripture, thinking that if they can exploit seeming "inconsistencies" or supposed "errors," they can somehow do away with Christianity and even God. That's the first mistake. Saying that "the Bible has some things I don't agree with, so the Church must be wrong and God, therefore, is "unloving" or "not real" (or whatever else) is completely backwards. Faith doesn't begin with the Bible. You don't use the Bible to prove God's existence . . . that's like using the music of Nikki Minaj or One Direction to "prove" that God hates me.

No, we begin with God. Once a soul believes in God, there's a decision to make regarding whether or not Jesus is God. Next, one must decide whether or not Christ instituted a Church or not. After that, one must understand that the Bible came out of a living Church (not vice versa). You can read more about this in the section on "Tradition." The Church didn't "come out of" the Bible; the Bible came out of Christ's Church.

> **God's Word, while timeless, offers timely wisdom for any circumstances or challenges we face.**

IN DEPTH:

The Scriptures are meant to be a light, and they are designed to not only guide us through darkness but also to beckon others to safety. The Scriptures reveal God's plan, speak truth, and challenge us to change. God's Word, while timeless, offers timely wisdom for any circumstances or challenges we face. Basically, the Father loved us so much that He gave us His Word (the compass) and His Church (the guide), refusing to orphan His children in a wilderness of sin and immorality.

Words Matter

Prepositions matter. We proclaim – as the early Christians did

– that the Bible is the *Word of God* . . . not merely words "about" God.

These words were written down (through the inspiration of the Holy Spirit) to communicate the truth of the events that had occurred and were occurring. St. Luke, by his own admission, was not an eyewitness (as Matthew and John were), but received the truth of the events from eyewitnesses and ministers (Luke 1:2).

The truth was too good not to share (Luke 1:4).

He was so taken by the inexplicable reality of what he heard and saw that he just had to write it down in an orderly way (Luke 1:3), to share this good news (the word "gospel" literally means "good news"). The truth was too good not to share (Luke 1:4). The question isn't why did they feel the need to share this with all they encountered, but why don't more people still have a passion to share it?

"Modern" Snobs

The next mistake is when modern minds get snobbish, saying that the Bible is "too outdated" or "not applicable" in our current culture. The idea that "old ideas" are not as solid as new ideas is not only stupid, it's dangerously prideful. Old ideas are often far better because they've held up over time.

If you claimed to know better than a group of people in the modern age, you'd sound like a snob; someone claiming to

The idea that "old ideas" are not as solid as new ideas is not only stupid, it's dangerously prideful.

"know better" than a group of people from the past really isn't any different. Yes, maybe you have the Internet, but they knew how to build pyramids without cranes, harvest crops without tractors, heal without prescriptions, and chart stars without telescopes.

Angels are Not Fairies

Some people try to dismiss the Bible because they say it's all just fairy tales and myths. Not only are they denying the eyewitness accounts of countless souls who saw loaves multiply or the dead raised or the sea part, but they are also confusing different types of storytelling. Allegory was a popular form of storytelling, for instance. When the writers of Scripture – led and inspired by the Holy Spirit – used allegories as moral parables, they communicated truth to us, even if the truth was not literal.

The Church doesn't teach that you have to believe God created everything in six 24-hour periods, but she does teach that everything was created by God with purpose. While the stories of creation may not be "scientifically accurate" as some scholarly types like to point out, it's important to point out that Genesis was not written as a scientific textbook. The author(s) of Genesis sought to explain "why" God created, not the "how." Saying Genesis scientifically proves God doesn't exist is like saying my love letter to my wife doesn't prove that I exist – or that the phone book doesn't prove that gravity is true; that was never their intended purpose!

The author(s) of Genesis sought to explain "why" God created, not the "how."

Now, that's not to say that everything in the Bible is allegorical... far from it. When Jesus healed the blind man, that literally happened. When He multiplied the loaves, again, that literally happened. You can take additional symbolic or sacramental meaning out of those miracles, which only enhance the physical, literal truth of the action. It's not an "either/or" but a "both/and" kind of miracle.

Finding Yourself in Scripture
Given all of this, some still wonder why we even need the Bible anymore. I mean, if we have our common sense, a conscience, and we have the Church, isn't the Bible – with all its ancient cultural references and accepted "ways of life" – kind of unnecessary?

If anything, we need the Bible more than ever before. It's dangerous to live in any present moment where you have forgotten your past. What if the God you "think" you know isn't the actual God at all? Many people follow a concept of Jesus that is not historically accurate – a pleasant, politically correct, "be nice to everyone" figure of Jesus that is anything but Biblical. Many people ascribe traits to God that are not even remotely consistent with the God of Scripture.

In the Bible you encounter the God of the Universe and see how He moves, thinks, and speaks. You're not merely reading about characters from long ago – you're reading about your very self. The Bible isn't merely speaking to you; it's speaking about you.

You are Adam and Eve, standing before God in all of your sin. You are Moses, worried about his reputation as he strikes the rock a second time. You are David, putting your wants before God's. You are Esther, deciding whether or not to endanger yourself to protect others. You are Peter, being called to lead even though you're far from perfect. You are the woman caught in adultery, or the woman at the well, or Zacchaeus – being told, by God, that you have worth regardless of your past.

In the Bible you encounter the God of the Universe and see how He moves, thinks and speaks. You're not merely reading about characters from long ago – you're reading about your very self.

This is what the Bible offers you... an invitation to know God more deeply. The Bible helps you to "know" God beyond just your head and to engage Him in your heart. Scripture deepens your prayer, enlivens your worship, and makes the sacraments come to life in a whole new way.

SUGGESTED READING:

CCC 106-07, 111, 133, 2653
Alan Schreck, *The Essential Catholic Catechism*
Scott Hahn, *Reasons to Believe*

WHAT IS TRADITION, AND HOW DOES IT RELATE TO THE BIBLE?

IN BRIEF:

Imagine your friend came to you and asked if you wanted to go with him to meet the Pope in Rome. You excitedly respond, "Yes!" and ask when you're leaving. Your friend then proceeds to tell you that he rented a plane to fly you both there, and that he just finished reading a book teaching him how to fly. Although your friend has never flown a plane before and has never had a lesson from a pilot, he feels confident after reading the book that he can do it. Would you fly with him?

While a book about flying might contain all of the truths and facts, the "how to" you need to know, it's not the same as sitting with a pilot in the cockpit and watching him or her do everything they do, "hands on." In a similar way, while the Bible is absolute truth and free of all error - introducing you to the story of salvation and your place in it - the Christian faith is a lived experience, as part of the larger Church that Christ, Himself, instituted. Tradition in the Catholic Church is the passing of truth to those who are learning about the faith, which we all are. Tradition can be taught by spoken word or can be written down. We learn not only from the Tradition that the Holy Spirit inspired (Scripture), but also from the Tradition that the Holy Spirit guides and protects (the Church) in all of its teachings (John 14:25-26, 16:13).

IN DEPTH:

When the Church speaks about "Tradition" it can mean a couple of different things. There is the oral tradition – things that were spoken and taught from Christ and His apostles to disciples and crowds – and the written tradition handed down in Gospels and books and letters, years (decades, actually) after the Resurrection. St. Paul reminded St. Timothy that the Bible is indispensable in our formation and incredibly useful (2 Timothy 3:16), but it's not the only source we learn from (1 Timothy 3:15).

In the first years of the Church, the people who referred to themselves as Christian had no New Testament. It had not yet been written, so early Christians lived by the word of mouth that was passed from one small community to the next (2 Corinthians 11:2; 2 Thessalonians 3:6). We hear about the apostles preaching to different churches in different areas of the world. St. Paul actually tells the Thessalonians to remember what they were taught by word of mouth and by the letters written to them (2 Thessalonians 2:15). Jesus, Himself never asked the apostles to write anything but to simply preach that He had risen from the dead and to baptize all nations in the name of the Trinity (Matthew 28:19). In fact, the only writing Jesus ever does is in the dirt (John 8:8).

In the first years of the Church, the people who referred to themselves as Christian had no New Testament. It had not yet been written, so early Christians lived by the word of mouth that was passed from one small community to the next (2 Corinthians 11:2; 2 Thessalonians 3:6).

The oral tradition – the preaching and its reception – was the foundation of the early Church. "Faith comes from what is heard," we are reminded in Scripture (Romans 10:17). The Church preached and the people believed (1 Corinthians 15:3, 11). The word of the Lord, which "abides forever," was preached (1 Peter 1:25). In fact, the very last thing St. John tells us in his Gospel is that " there are also many other things which Jesus did; were every one of them to be written, I suppose that the world itself could not contain the books that would be written" (John 21:25). The Gospel, itself, tells us that there is more to (the Christian) life than just the Gospels. Again, this is not to say that the oral tradition is "more important" than the written, not at all; they are complementary not contradictory.

Later, as the Scriptures came to be accepted by the Church, Tradition assumed its full written form. What started with the tradition of the Old Testament was completed in the New Testament! That Tradition continued to be opened and expanded by those who had been given the authority to do so: the apostles and their chosen successors, the bishops. We are told that the early Christians "devoted themselves to the apostles' teaching" (Acts 2:42). The teaching authority of the Church is known as the Magisterium. Collectively, the written and oral Traditions, and the Magisterium form a three-legged stool, sturdy enough to support two thousand years of Catholic history and over one billion Catholics worldwide.

SUGGESTED READINGS:

CCC 75-79, 81, 84, 97, 174, 126, 1124
Alan Schreck, *The Compact History of the Catholic Church*
Peter Kreeft, *Fundamentals of the Faith*

WHO WROTE THE BIBLE?

IN BRIEF:

Put simply, the Holy Spirit is the ultimate author of the Scriptures. An easy way to think of it is the Holy Spirit writing "through" the different writers – they were pens in God's hand. The Bible consists of 73 books, penned by 40 to 50 writers over about 1,700 years. It would take an hour just to collect all of those signatures. The reality would be that while the writers were responsible for putting pen to parchment, it is the Holy Spirit who inspired the words; God is the author of Scripture.

IN DEPTH:

Some people have a difficult time with the idea that God is the ultimate author of the Bible. It's safer and more convenient to say that people were writing about God, rather than acknowledging the truth – the Bible is the Living Word of God (Hebrews 4:12). Scripture isn't people writing "their take" about God, but rather God breathing words through the pens of men. Did God utilize the different talents and gifts for writing, communication, and storytelling of each author? Absolutely. He used their gifts the same way He still uses peoples' gifts in ministry every day.

> No other work in the present or in the future, no matter how brilliant, will be held in the same esteem as the Gospels; they are *that* divine, *that* perfect.

The Bible is without error. It is the fullness of God's revelation. That does not mean we understand all of it. Over the centuries, the Holy Spirit continues to illuminate us with new depths of truth, deeper avenues into the heart of God through His Word. God is constantly revealing Himself to us in deeper ways. When people say that Scripture is the "fullness of revelation," it means that no other books or writings since the Bible can or would be held in the same esteem. The Bible was inspired in a unique way, at a unique time in God's plan of salvation and in history. No other work in the present or in the future, no matter how brilliant, will be held in the same esteem as the Gospels; they are *that* divine, *that* perfect.

The word "canon" means, "measuring rod." Canon is the term used to describe which Biblical books "measured up" and were included in what we now call the Holy Bible. So the canon is the "official" list of which books made the cut, so to speak. We discuss the canon in more detail when we talk about why the Catholic and Protestant Bibles are slightly different on page 94.

While the Old Testament was already written and compiled before the baby Jesus was put in the manger, there were hundreds of written works to be considered when compiling the New Testament canon. Dozens of "gospels" began to make their way around, each with their own unique spin on the life of Christ, some accurate, most absolutely inauthentic.

Lastly, it was the universal (Catholic) Christian Church who finally put the Scriptures together in the form you know today. It took years to formalize the full canon of Scripture.

There are a few important things to note here:

First, the New Testament was almost entirely oral tradition (shared through speech, not writing) in the years immediately following Jesus' death. We discuss this more in the question about Tradition on page 84.

Second, the writers of the New Testament belonged to the only Church Christ founded (they were Catholic) and they believed in the True Presence of Christ in the Eucharist, including St. Paul (1 Corinthians 10:16-31) who wasn't even at the Last Supper, but who was taught about Christ's sacraments through oral tradition.

Lastly, it was the universal (Catholic) Christian Church who finally put the Scriptures together in the form you know today. It took years to formalize the full canon of Scripture. Travel was difficult back then, communication was slow, transcription was costly, Christianity was deadly, and the Church was exploding in growth. It took many years of prayer, conversation, discernment, and debate by bishops, scholars, and leaders to prayerfully determine (through the guidance of the Author, the Holy Spirit) which Biblical books were truly inspired. That process of prayer, guided by the Spirit, gave us the commonly held canon.

Any non-canonical or heretical books were disregarded, for the most part, over time. Finally, at the Councils of Rome (382 A.D.),

Hippo (393 A.D.), and Carthage (397 A.D.) the list of inspired books was set. It's the same list you hold in your hands (when you hold a Catholic Bible, that is) today. The Council of Trent (1545-1563) promulgated the canon for us, but the canon was commonly held for well over a thousand years before even that.

SUGGESTED READING:

CCC 78-97, 120-138, 106-107
Alan Schreck, *The Compact History of the Catholic Church*
Dave Armstrong, *The Catholic Verses*
Scott Hahn, *Spirit & Life*

IS THE BIBLE SEXIST?

IN BRIEF:
The answer is, "No." The Bible is not sexist. This is a somewhat common misperception that has been around for a long time and will probably continue to be around for a couple reasons:

1. People misunderstanding passages.

2. People not addressing the reasons some think the Bible is sexist.

Did the Bible take place during a time in history and spring forth from cultures that largely treated women with little or no dignity? Yes, in many cases. That being said, the Bible is the inspired Word of God and must be viewed and studied through a higher perspective than our own modern culture or personal ideologies. Many who personally "find" the Bible sexist are viewing it looking to prove their own opinion, which is called *eisegesis*; it is an improper reading of Scripture. Eisegesis "reads into" Scripture with our own preconceived ideologies and perceptions. We are called to read Scripture through an approach called *exegesis* (meaning "to guide out"). Through exegesis we "read out of" the Bible the proper intention of God, taking into account a passage's cultural context, the date of composition, literary structures and word play, notes about the book's author and audience, translation challenges and so on. Proper interpretation of the Bible takes time and great attention to detail, free of pride, attitude, or personal beliefs – no matter how seemingly valid.

IN DEPTH:
It is difficult to treat this type of a broad stroke accusation without a specific verse to work through. As mentioned above, the context of a passage is essential to understand its intended meaning.

For our purposes here, let's take a passage like the one below:

> "[...] the women should keep silence in the churches. For they are not permitted to speak, but should be subordinate, as even the

law says. If there is anything they desire to know, let them ask their husbands at home. For it is shameful for a woman to speak in church."

- 1 Corinthians 14:34-35

Upon a quick or cursory reading of a passage such as this one, almost any modern reader could quickly judge St. Paul to be sexist and – by extension – the Bible to be almost misogynistic. People then say, "Well, that's the way culture was back then... women didn't have any rights." The problem with leaving it like that is that it makes some people say to themselves, "Well, then the Bible is out-of-date," or "I can pick and choose which passages apply to me and throw the rest out as irrelevant." It leaves God's inspired Word up to one's own personal judgment and asserts that the Bible has errors. Both of those conclusions are incorrect and highly dangerous to our walk as Christians.

If we took a closer look at the section, and if we understood better what was going on in the churches in Corinth at the time, these words of St. Paul would not be seen so much as "sexist," but as practical and necessary because of the situation.

You see, during this time the assemblies at church in Corinth were getting really "carried away" with the worship, and were easily swept up into the emotion of the Spirit, without any strong faith formation, not rooted in prayer (kind of like – all fluff and no substance).

St. Paul was trying to give them some practical suggestions to help them keep order and depth in their worship. This is why reading only a verse or two (as excerpted above) and not the entire passage can be dangerous.

If you open your Bible and read the verses prior, you'll notice that before he talks about women in verses 34-35, he also gives specific directives to people about speaking in tongues (27-28) and prophesying (29-33). Further, as we can see from 1 Corinthians 11:5, St. Paul is **not at all** against women prophesying; he is just trying to help the church leaders keep a spirit of respect and reverence during their preaching and worship.

If someone says to you that St. Paul is "sexist" or a "chauvinist," politely tell that person that the Bible is anything but sexist. In fact, St. Paul is foundationally and supremely concerned about the equality of men and women as children of God. That is not to say that men and women don't have different roles within God's plan of salvation (they do, very different), but **neither role is more important than the other.**

People who are threatened by an all-male priesthood, for instance, should strive to remember that in the Kingdom of heaven, it is the **saints** not the ordained ministers, who are the greatest. Many of our greatest saints are women! In fact, we ought never forget that the Queen of heaven, the Blessed Virgin Mary, is a woman.

That is not to say that men and women don't have different roles within God's plan of salvation (they do, very different), but neither role is more important than the other.

So, why do these misconceptions occur? Well, don't be too hard on people who are quick to label or judge something as sexist. People can be, but God is not. Sometimes it's as simple as a problem with translation(s). We must remember that we are reading translations of translations when we read the Bible. Often times there will be a phrase that doesn't translate the idiom (an expression known to a specific group at a specific time) as cleanly a couple of thousand years after it was uttered. Translations are forced to capture the intention and not just the material. The modern day perception of the Bible as "sexist," for instance, usually comes from people with good intentions, but poor formation.

In Christ we have a portrait of a man who has the highest respect for women, constantly lifting them up and revealing their dignity to all (John 4:4-28, 8:2-11). Since when we see Christ "we see the Father" (John 14:7-11), we can rest in full confidence that not only does God celebrate women, but one could say that God is their biggest fan. His children ought to celebrate womanhood just as He does.

The only "sexist" thing about the Bible is when Christian men don't live out the Gospel toward the women in their life, and when Christian women don't live out the Gospel toward the men in theirs.

In Christ we have a portrait of a man who has the highest respect for women, constantly lifting them up and revealing their dignity to all (John 4:4-28, 8:2-11).

SUGGESTED READING:

Dale Ahlquist, *Common Sense 101: Lessons from G. K. Chesterton*, Chapter XI
Peter Kreeft, *You Can Understand the Bible*

WHY DO CATHOLICS AND PROTESTANTS HAVE DIFFERENT BIBLES? WHY DO PROTESTANT BIBLES HAVE FEWER BOOKS?

IN BRIEF:

People will often accuse the Catholic Church of *adding* books to the Bible. That's not only untrue, but the person who says it is not someone you'd want to help you study for that history midterm. You'd be better off on your own because history is apparently not their strong suit. It is true that the Catholic Bible has more books (73) than the Protestant Bible (66). Both have 27 Books in the New Testament; it's the Old Testament that there is a disagreement over.

The books in question (again, from the Old Testament) are Tobit, Judith, Wisdom, Sirach (Ecclesiasticus), Baruch, I and II Maccabees, and parts of Esther and Daniel. Since the Bible we have today did not fall out of the sky neatly bound in leather, it is important to look at where it came from historically and why the Catholic Church teaches that the 73 book translation of the Sacred Scriptures is not only preferable but fully inspired.

The Septuagint was the Old Testament that the New Testament writers most frequently used as a reference when they wrote their individual books (there are over 300 allusions to the Septuagint in the New Testament but only about 30 from the Hebrew canon).

IN DEPTH:

So why does the Catholic Bible have 46 Old Testament books when our Protestant brothers and sisters have the "lighter" 39 book version? As was just discussed in the section on "Who wrote the Bible?" (on page 87) it comes down to the canon.

First, you need to understand that there are two different canons of the Old Testament: the Palestinian Canon (the Protestant Old Testament) and the Alexandrian Canon (the Catholic Old Testament). The Palestinian Canon was written in Hebrew and the Alexandrian Canon in Greek. So which one did Jesus "use"?

By the time Jesus was born, Hebrew was becoming a dead language; Jesus, for instance, spoke Aramaic (as did most Palestinian Jews). As the Greek language became the more dominant and more widely used, a translation of the Hebrew Bible into Greek (called the Septuagint) was created by 70 Jewish scholars between 250-125 B.C.; the word "septuagint" is Latin for seventy.

People will often accuse the Catholic Church of adding books to the Bible, but as you can see, it was a group of Jewish rabbis who removed books from the Bible, and Martin Luther who accepted this removal of books.

So by the time that Christ was born, Greek was the common language of the Mediterranean world and the Septuagint was very popular. Jesus would have been very familiar with the Septuagint, along with all of the New Testament writers. In fact, the Septuagint was the Old Testament that the New Testament writers most frequently used as a reference when they wrote their individual books (there are over 300 allusions to the Septuagint in the New Testament but only about 30 from the Hebrew canon). We cannot forget, either, that the New Testament was written in Greek.

This canon of the Old Testament – the Alexandrian Canon of 46 books - was accepted as the canon for 1,500 years, until the Protestant Reformation. In 1529, Martin Luther (a Catholic priest who became the leader of the Protestant Reformation) decided to use the Palestinian Canon (39 books) as his Old Testament canon.

People will often accuse the Catholic Church of *adding* books to the Bible, but as you can see, it was a group of Jewish rabbis who *removed* books from the Bible, and Martin Luther who accepted this removal of books. In fact, Luther wanted to remove even more books from the Bible, the Book of James and Revelation, which is *unbiblical* to do (Deuteronomy 4:2; Revelation 22:18-19).

What you should ask yourself is whether you would rather use the Old Testament canon quoted, referred to, and read by the apostles and New Testament writers or the Old Testament compiled by a group of Jews who later rejected Christ?

To put it simply, when you're holding the Catholic Bible, you're holding the original, the Director's Cut, with all the footage and all the special features; the non-Catholic translations are like the films that are resized and edited to fit your screen or the network timeslot.

SUGGESTED READING:

CCC 120, 138, 81, 106-107
Mark Shea, *Making Senses out of Scripture*
Scott Hahn, *Reasons to Believe*
Dave Armstrong, *The Catholic Verses*
Alan Schreck, *The Compact History of the Catholic Church*

THE CHURCH

WHERE DID THE CATHOLIC CHURCH COME FROM?
I LOVE JESUS, BUT DO I REALLY NEED THE CHURCH?

IN BRIEF:

The Catholic Church was founded by Jesus Christ with the twelve apostles as the foundation. It was to them that Jesus entrusted His saving message. Just as He was sent by the Father to save us from sin and teach us how to live, the apostles were sent by Jesus to continue His saving mission throughout history. It is through these twelve (the foundation of the Church) that the world has come to hear the good news of the Gospel. You and I would not know who Jesus was if it weren't for the Church that made sure His message was preserved and shared over the past 2000 years. Do we need the Church? Yes. Why? Because Jesus set it up that way.

IN DEPTH:

Many Christians say that they love Jesus, that they accept Him as their Lord and savior, and seek to follow Him in all that they do. This is great; this is what our relationship with Jesus is supposed to look like. The problem is that many

The word "church" can have three different meanings.

of these same people would also say that they don't need any church as a part of this relationship. While they might say that it is nice to have a community to belong to, to have a group of like-minded people to help support and encourage them in their walk with God, many of them would say they don't actually need a church; and this is a big problem.

Why? Because the Church was established by Jesus to be a continuation of His mission, so a rejection of the Church is ultimately a rejection of Christ who established the Church. Now, before we explain this, let me briefly define what we mean by "church." The word "church" can have three different meanings.

First it can refer to a building, the place where Christians gather for prayer and worship. It can also refer to the community of believers, to those people around the world who follow Christ and so are united by a common bond. But it can also refer to the institution that leads and governs all the people of God. Now, there is no problem with "church" as a building where Christians gather or with understanding "church" as a group of believers throughout the world. (All Christians would generally agree that having a place to gather is a good thing, and most accept some understanding of some kind of unity between fellow Christians called "church.") The real issue here is over the question of "church" as an institution, "Church" with a capital C. When it comes to the idea of a "Church" as an institution (with leadership, structure, rules, etc.), many Christians draw the line. They would say that Jesus never intended for there to be a "church" in this sense. But if this is the case, then where did this "Church" come from? And if we love Jesus, do we really need this Church (with a capital C)?

Now, before answering this question, can we admit that *if* a Church does exist that was established by Christ to continue His work, this Church would be pretty important, right? And *if* there is an institution that was given the mission and authority to lead the followers of Christ until He comes again, listening to what this Church has to say would be pretty important as well, right? It would certainly seem so. So, the question is this: Did Jesus establish such a Church? And if so, where is it?

The answer to the first question is yes, Jesus did establish a Church, and this Church was meant to continue His work of reconciling us to God and teaching us how to live. As for the second question, well, this Church is the Catholic Church founded nearly 2000 years ago by Jesus Himself. How do we know?

If we look at how Jesus related to the apostles throughout His ministry, we see that He was gathering a specific group from among all of His followers who He was going to set up as leaders of the community after He went back to the Father. We can see this in the fact that from among all of His *disciples,* He chose twelve men whom He called *apostles* (sometimes referred to as *the twelve*). From among all of the people who followed Him (the disciples) Jesus chose twelve particular men for a specific role and purpose within the community (the apostles). It was to these apostles that Jesus gave the mission of teaching and baptizing in His name and with His authority. What is interesting about this is that Jesus repeatedly says throughout the Gospels that He was sent by the Father to do the work of the Father. The mission of Jesus is ultimately rooted in the will of the Father who sent Him. But this is the exact same pattern that we see with Jesus and the apostles. Just as Jesus was sent by the Father to do His work, the apostles are sent forth by Jesus to continue His work. In fact, Jesus says exactly this when He appears to the twelve after His Resurrection: "As the Father has sent me, so I send you" (John 20:21).

What we see here is a sort of continuation of the original mission. God had a plan to save us and bring us back into communion with Himself. To accomplish this, He sent His own Son who came to do the work of the One who sent Him. Jesus, throughout His life, selects twelve men from among His followers and entrusts to them the mission of continuing what He has begun. The apostles (like Jesus) do not go out on their own but are sent by Jesus with His authority and with a mission received from Him. These twelve apostles are the foundation of the Catholic Church which has continued from the apostles to the pope and bishops that we have today. (For more on this, check out the next question.) Just as Jesus said that those who reject Him are also rejecting the one who sent Him (the Father), He also tells the apostles that He sends forth that "whoever receives the one I send receives me" (John 13:20).

So where does all of this leave us? We know that Jesus came with a mission to save us from sin and teach us how to live. This mission was given to Him by the Father who sent Him. Did Jesus accomplish this task? Of course. Through His teaching and especially through His death and Resurrection, Jesus provides us with a way back to the Father; but this way had to be shown to the entire world, and to do this Jesus sent forth twelve men. Twelve men who had received a mission from Jesus and the power to carry it out through the Holy Spirit. These twelve are the foundation of the Church (with a big "C"). They are the ones who were entrusted with Jesus' saving Gospel. To say that we love Jesus, but that we don't need the Church really doesn't make any sense.

Were it not for the Church (which began with the ministry of the apostles), we would have never even heard of Jesus. It is through the Church that Jesus was made known to the world. He continues to be made known through the Church today through the pope and bishops of the Catholic Church (which is the topic of our next question).

SUGGESTED READING:

Dei Verbum, Chapter II
Lumen Gentium, Chapter III
John 13-17
Fr. Robert Barron, *Catholicism: A Journey to the Heart of the Faith*
Peter Kreeft, *Catholic Christianity*

THINGS TO CONSIDER:

Jesus unites [the apostles] to the mission He received from the Father. As 'the Son can do nothing of His own accord,' but receives everything from the Father who sent Him, so those whom Jesus sends can do nothing apart from Him, from whom they received both the mandate for their mission and the power to carry it out" (CCC 859).

"Jesus Christ, the eternal pastor, set up the holy Church by entrusting the apostles with their mission as He, Himself, had been sent by the Father" (Lumen Gentium, 18).

"God graciously arranged that the things He had once revealed for the salvation of all people should remain in their entirety, throughout the ages, and be transmitted to all generations. Therefore, Christ the Lord, in whom the entire Revelation of the most high God is summed up commanded the apostles to preach the Gospel [...] This was faithfully done: it was done by the apostles who handed on, by the spoken word of their preaching, by the example they gave, by the institutions they established, what they themselves had received — whether from the lips of Christ, from His way of life and His works, or whether they had learned it at the prompting of the Holy Spirit" (Dei Verbum, 7).

WHAT IS THE RELATIONSHIP BETWEEN THE APOSTLES AND THE BISHOPS WE HAVE TODAY?

IN BRIEF:

The bishops of the Catholic Church are the direct successors of the twelve apostles. When the Church first began, the apostles were given the mission and the authority to spread the Gospel. As they did this, they set up leaders within each community who would continue to lead the people as the apostles had done. These first successors were the presbyters (or bishops) of the early Church. Over time, the authority that they had received from the apostles was passed down to those who were left in charge of guiding the people according to the teachings of Christ and the apostles sent forth by Him. This process continued all the way down to today, so that the bishops of our time are connected to the first apostles through an unbroken chain, which the Church calls *apostolic succession.*

IN DEPTH:

Before we answer this question, we need to make sure that we understand the difference between an *apostle* and a *disciple*, since these words are not interchangeable. The disciples were those men and women who followed Jesus and sought to live according to His teaching. This was true then and it is true today; all of us who seek to faithfully follow Jesus can rightly be called *disciples* of Christ. The apostles, on the other hand, were twelve men specifically chosen by Jesus from among all of His followers. From among the disciples, Jesus chose twelve whom He named apostles. The twelve apostles were given a specific task to teach in Jesus' name and to make known all that they had received from Him. The disciples were those who responded to Jesus' invitation to follow Him and live according to the way of the Gospel.

The apostles were those followers of Christ who were given a unique share in Jesus' mission of reconciling us to the Father and teaching us how to live. So while all of the apostles were disciples, not all of the disciples were apostles. Within the early Church, the twelve apostles were recognized as having a unique place and role among all of Jesus' followers.

Now, strictly speaking, the word "apostle" means *one who is sent*; an apostle can be anyone that is sent by Jesus for a specific task. This is why the Church refers to St. Paul as an apostle; when Jesus appeared to him, St. Paul was sent out with a specific mission (see Acts 9). The Church has traditionally used the word "apostle" to refer to those men that Jesus sent out with the specific mission of continuing to teach and preach in His name (see Matthew 28:16-20). Those twelve, with Peter as their head, were the first to preach the Gospel in Jesus' name, and they formed the first Christian communities. They were recognized in the early Church as having the unique role of spreading Jesus' saving message.

We can see this, for example, if we look at the Acts of the Apostles, where Peter stands up after Pentecost and gives the first recorded proclamation of the Gospel. After going through God's plan of saving us through the life and ministry of Jesus, Peter says, "Therefore let the whole house of Israel know for certain that God has made Him both Lord and Messiah, this Jesus whom you crucified" (Acts 2:36). In response to Peter's preaching, many people were baptized and began to follow Christ.

So, the apostles were the foundation of the early Church (as we said, by the way, in the last question). That's all fine and good, but the next question that people naturally ask is, "what do these twelve have to do with the bishops in the Church today?"

Well, the answer to this question is found by looking at how the Church began to spread immediately after the apostles began their mission on Pentecost. The apostles would go from town to town proclaiming the Gospel and forming those who accepted their message into a community of believers. As they did this, the apostles would appoint certain people as leaders within those communities (Acts 14:23), "faithful people who will have the ability to teach others" (2 Timothy 2:2). The task that the apostles had received from Jesus would be passed on to others who would continue to guide the Christian community with the authority of the apostles, an authority that they had themselves received from Jesus. These leaders (which the New Testament calls presbyters or elders and who functioned as bishops) were appointed to this role through what the New Testament calls the laying on of hands (or the imposition of hands). What we see happening here is that the authority, initially given by Jesus to the apostles, was being handed on to others who would unite themselves to that same mission to go and make disciples of all nations.

In the same way, as the community continued to grow and as time passed, this same authority that was handed on from the apostles to their first successors was passed on to others as well. These "others" (who were the successors of that first generation of successors) were the bishops of the early Church, and this process continued from them all the way down to the bishops that we have today. This passing of apostolic authority throughout history is called apostolic succession.

So what is the relationship between the apostles and the bishops today? It is a direct link. The bishops today are the successors (over many generations) of the first apostles. There is an unbroken chain that connects our current bishops to the first twelve apostles. This link is so strong that Jesus' words to the apostles can rightly be applied to our own bishops today: "As the Father has sent me, so I send you" (John 20:21), and "Whoever listens to you listens to me. Whoever rejects you rejects me" (Luke 10:16).

SUGGESTED READING:

CCC 857-865
Dei Verbum, Chapter II
Lumen Gentium, Chapter III
Patrick Madrid, *Pope Fiction*

THINGS TO CONSIDER:

> *"They devoted themselves to the teaching of the apostles and to the communal life, to the breaking of the bread and to the prayers. Awe came upon everyone, and many wonders and signs were done through the apostles" (Acts 2:42-43).*

> *"In order that the full and living Gospel might always be preserved in the Church, the apostles left bishops as their successors. They gave them 'their own position of teaching authority'" (Dei Verbum, 7).*

> *"Do not neglect the gift you have, which was conferred on you through the prophetic word with the imposition of hands of the presbyterate" (1 Timothy 4:14).*

"In order that the mission entrusted to them might be continued after their death, they consigned, by will and testament, as it were, to their immediate collaborators the duty of completing and consolidating the work they had begun, urging them to tend to the whole flock, in which the Holy Spirit had appointed them to shepherd the Church of God" (Lumen Gentium, 20).

"The apostolic tradition is manifested and preserved in the whole world by those who were made bishops by the apostles and by their successors down to our own time" (Lumen Gentium, 20).

Apostolic succession: "The handing on of apostolic preaching and authority from the apostles to their successors the bishops through the laying on of hands, as a permanent office in the Church" (CCC Glossary).

WHAT DOES IT MEAN TO SAY THAT THE "FULLNESS OF TRUTH" IS FOUND IN THE CATHOLIC CHURCH?

IN BRIEF:
Jesus came to reveal to us the truth about who God is and how we are to live in relationship to Him. This truth was entrusted to the apostles and through their successors (the pope and bishops of the Church today) the Catholic Church continues to make known to the world the fullness of divine Revelation. And so, although truth (even Christian truth) can be found outside of the Catholic Church, it is only through the Church that the *fullness* of divine Revelation can be known with certainty.

IN DEPTH:
This is one of those things that is often misunderstood by those outside of the Church (and honestly, by many within the Church as well). It might sound like the Church is saying that truth can only be found in the Catholic Church, and that anything outside of Catholicism cannot be trusted as true. Now this is certainly not the case. The Church recognizes that the human mind is capable of knowing many things without the help of the Church. In fact, this is even true of many religious truths, such as the existence of God. The Church recognizes that many people have been able to discover the existence of God by using human reason alone. So, this idea of the Church as the "fullness of truth" cannot be understood as a claim to a sort of monopoly on truth, as if no truth could be found outside Church teaching.

So what does it mean? It means that the truth that Jesus came to reveal was entrusted, in all its fullness, to the Catholic Church. When it comes to those things that God wished to make known to us for our salvation (which is called divine Revelation), the *fullness* of this truth is found in the teachings of the Catholic Church, which was established by Jesus to pass on this truth in all its fullness throughout history. Let's use the analogy of a movie. Let's suppose that an entire movie represents all that God has revealed to us through Jesus Christ. Now, this movie (I mean, Revelation) was given to the Church to be shared with the entire world. But it is only through watching the *entire movie* that you will be able to really understand what it is about. If you have only parts of the movie, you might get some good stuff, but you won't understand the whole story. If all you see of a movie is unconnected scenes, you might be able to follow the story, but you won't understand all of the details of the story.

Well, a similar thing is true of divine Revelation. Throughout history, God has chosen to reveal Himself to us. He did this in the Old Testament through people like Abraham, Moses, and the prophets, but He revealed Himself most fully through His own Son. In Jesus, we see everything that God wanted to reveal to us about Himself, about who we are, and about how to share in His own divine life by grace. Jesus is the way, the truth, and the life; in the life and teachings of Jesus, God has made Himself known in an entirely unique way.

Now this Revelation – this fullness of truth – that Jesus came to give us was entrusted to the Church. This means that the Church today has the task of making this truth known to the world. Through the Church, Jesus' saving truth continues to be revealed to the world. So it is the Church that has the full movie (going back to our analogy before). It is through the Church that the whole story is shown to the world.

But what about those Christians who are not Catholic? Ever since the Protestant Reformation in the 15th century, Christianity has been divided, so that now there are many non-Catholic Christian churches. Now the Church recognizes that there is a lot within these Christian groups that is good and true. However, the Protestant Reformation led to a lot of these groups abandoning much of what made up that original Revelation entrusted to the apostles (such as the nature of the Church and the meaning of the sacraments). This means that some of these non-Catholic Christian communities don't have the whole picture; they don't know the full story because they are missing scenes from the movie. And so, while there might be much in them that is true, the *fullness* of Christian truth is found only in the Catholic Church. This is because it was to the Catholic Church, founded upon the teaching of the apostles, that the fullness of Christ's Revelation was entrusted.

Although truth (even Christian truth) does exist and can be found outside of the Catholic Church, the fullness of God's saving truth is found in and through the teaching of the Catholic Church.

SUGGESTED READING:

Lumen Gentium, Chapter I
Unitatis Redintegratio
Peter Kreeft, *Fundamentals of the Faith*
G. K. Chesterton, *Orthodoxy*

THINGS TO CONSIDER:

"God communicates Himself to man gradually. He prepares Him to welcome by stages the supernatural Revelation that is to culminate in the person and mission of the incarnate Word, Jesus Christ" (CCC 53).

Jesus said, "Whoever has seen me has seen the Father" (John 14:9).

"What was handed on by the apostles comprises everything that serves to make the People of God live their lives in holiness and increase their faith. In this way the Church in her doctrine, life and worship, perpetuates and transmits to every generation all that she herself is, all that she believes" (Dei Verbum, 8).

"It is through Christ's Catholic Church alone, which is the universal help towards salvation, that the fullness of the means of salvation can be obtained" (Unitatis Redintegratio, 3).

The Second Vatican Council states that although "many elements of sanctification and of truth are found outside of its visible confines," the one Church of Christ "subsists in the Catholic Church, which is governed by the successor of Peter and by the bishops in communion with him" (Lumen Gentium, 8).

WHY AREN'T PRIESTS MARRIED?
IS THAT IN THE BIBLE?

IN BRIEF:

Nowhere in the Bible does it say that priests must be unmarried. In fact, there have been times in the Church where priests have been married. But the Church has determined that, at this point in time, having celibate (unmarried) priests would best serve the needs of the Church. This practice of priests not being married is a *discipline* of the Church, and disciplines can be changed as the Church determines what is best for the current circumstances. So, while it doesn't say in the Bible that priests should not be married, it also doesn't say that they must be married, and there are even some places where being unmarried is seen as beneficial for those ministering within the Church (for example, check out Matthew 19:1-12 and 1 Corinthians 7:32-35).

IN DEPTH:

It actually doesn't say anywhere in the Bible that priests are not to be married, and we know that at least St. Peter was married. (Matthew 8:14-15 tells us about Jesus healing Peter's mother-in-law from an illness.) In fact, there have been many priests and bishops in the Church who were married, so there is nothing in the Bible that specifically forbids priests from being married. Well then, what's the deal, why aren't priests married today?

Over time, the Church came to feel that it would be in the best interest of priests, individual Catholics, priests' possible wives and children, etc. for priests not to be married. It was determined that for practical reasons, a celibate (meaning, unmarried) clergy (priesthood) would better serve the Church. However, it is important to realize that this is a *discipline* of the Church, not a requirement of the faith. There are many things in the Church that are disciplines, such as rules about fasting and about the language used during Mass. These disciplines are not the same as doctrines. Doctrines are part of divine Revelation and cannot be changed (examples would be the Church's teaching on Baptism as being necessary for salvation, or the Church's understanding of Jesus as fully human and fully divine). Doctrines cannot be changed but disciplines can.

So, at this point in the Church's history, the Church says that those seeking the Sacrament of Holy Orders (the sacrament by which men become priests) must be celibate. This is what the Church feels is most beneficial in our time, but it doesn't mean that this discipline could not change at some point in the future. This is really the main point we want you to get here: priests not being married is not a requirement of Catholic doctrine, it is a practice based upon the Church's judgment of what would be best for the Church in this time in history.

Now, it is true that this practice is something that people have a lot of mixed feelings about, and while going through all the arguments about this discipline is not the point, it is important to look at one spot in Scripture where Jesus talks about people sacrificing being married for the sake of the Kingdom of heaven. In Matthew 19:1-12 Jesus is being questioned about divorce, and toward the end of His response He says, "Some are incapable of marriage because they were born so; some, because they were made so by others; some, because they have renounced marriage for the sake of the Kingdom of heaven. Whoever can accept this ought to accept it" (Matthew 19:12). Jesus speaks of three different reasons why someone may not get married: the first two are due to factors outside of their control (either they have some birth defect or have been mutilated by another during their life), but the third is something that is done willingly. What Jesus is saying here is that there are some people who choose to give up marriage for the sake of devoting their entire life to serving and working for God's Kingdom.

Notice that Jesus says that not all people can accept this way of life, but that those who can accept it ought to accept it. This verse from Matthew is important for two reasons: one, because it shows that the idea of celibacy is not something that is unheard of in the Bible or in the teachings of Jesus, and two, because it reveals that God's call to the priesthood (which includes a call to celibacy) is not for all people, but only some. Those who are called to such a life ought to respond with faithful obedience.

The Church's discipline of having a celibate priesthood is not because the Church sees marriage as bad or as a hindrance to serving God. The Church recognizes both Matrimony and Holy Orders as ministries of the Church, both aimed at service and the building up of the Kingdom of God. But the Church also recognizes that being married places certain demands upon your time that could prevent you from being fully accessible for service to the Church. Imagine for example being a married priest at your daughter's high school graduation and getting a call to anoint someone dying in the hospital. What are you supposed to do? What takes priority?

A married man's time is not free for service only to the Church. He has obligations to his wife, his children, his job, etc. There is nothing wrong with these obligations, as they are part of the vocation to marriage; but an unmarried priest has the ability to devote himself wholeheartedly to the needs of the Church. Because of this, the Church has determined that unmarried clergy is the most suitable practice *at this point* in the Church's history.

SUGGESTED READING:
CCC 1577-1580
Fulton Sheen, *The Priest is Not His Own*

THINGS TO CONSIDER:

> *"All the ordained ministers of the Latin Church, with the exception of permanent deacons, are normally chosen from among men of faith who live a celibate life and who intend to remain celibate 'for the sake of the Kingdom of heaven'" (CCC 1579).*

> *"Called to consecrate themselves with undivided heart to the Lord and to 'the affairs of the Lord,' they give themselves entirely to God and to men" (CCC 1579).*

> *"Two other sacraments, Holy Orders and Matrimony, are directed towards the salvation of others [...] through these sacraments those already consecrated by Baptism and Confirmation for the common priesthood of all the faithful can receive particular consecrations. Those who receive the Sacrament of Holy Orders are consecrated in Christ's name 'to feed the Church by the word and grace of God.' On their part, 'Christian spouses are fortified and, as it were, consecrated for the duties and dignity of their state by a special sacrament'" (CCC 1534-1535).*

DOESN'T THE BIBLE SAY "CALL NO MAN FATHER"? SO, WHY DO CATHOLICS CALL PRIESTS FATHER?

IN BRIEF:

Referring to priests as "father" has been a practice of the Church since the earliest centuries of Christianity. St. Paul, for example, refers to himself having become "a father" to the Corinthians through the Gospel that he preached, see 1 Corinthians 4:15. When Jesus says that we are to call no one father, He is criticizing the improper exercise of authority by the Scribes and Pharisees (who liked these titles because they used them to set themselves up as better than others). Jesus is reminding those in positions of authority that leadership is found not in domination but in service, and service is at the heart of the priesthood. So when we call our priests "father," we are recognizing their role as spiritual guides, in the service of helping us to grow and mature as children of our true Father in heaven.

IN DEPTH:

Sometimes when this question is brought up (usually for the purpose of trying to discredit the Catholic Church), it seems that people think that Catholics have just never read Matthew 23:1-12, where Jesus does say that we are to call no man "father." Now, this is certainly not the case. The Church is well aware of these words of Jesus, and yet Catholic priests have been called "father" since the first centuries of the Church. So what's the deal? Is the Church just blatantly disregarding this verse?

It's important to point out that the very same verse also says that we are to call no man teacher, but for some reason it never seems to bother anyone that we go through years of school calling others "teacher." Also, if we were to really take this verse literally, we would never use the word "father" to refer to our own dads. So Jesus must be saying something else here, right? He isn't just asking for us to make a universal change from "father" and "teacher" to "dad" and "instructor" is He? It doesn't seem like there would be anything gained from just swapping out synonyms, (Jesus didn't just have a personal distaste for the words "father" and "teacher") so we need to look deeper to see what is really going on here.

In these verses, Jesus is speaking about the proper exercise of authority. This is clear from the fact that this teaching is given within the context of His criticizing the Scribes and Pharisees for their hypocrisy as teachers and leaders of the Jewish people. (Read all of Matthew 23; Jesus really lets them have it.) Many of the Scribes and Pharisees had developed a bad habit of dangling their power and authority over others. They loved having these titles of "father" and "teacher" because they were used to set themselves apart as superior to the rest of the Jews. And it is this practice of using their position as an opportunity to set themselves up as better than others that Jesus is rejecting.

Jesus is reminding us that authority ultimately comes from God and that those who have received a position of leadership should exercise this leadership not for their own benefit but for the good of others. When we seek titles like "father" and "teacher" for our own sake, we lose sight of the fact that God is the true teacher and father, and that those who are given a role of leadership must act in a way that humbly recognizes that greatness consists in serving others, not in seeking your own glory and benefit.

We can see that what Jesus is criticizing here is not the title itself, but those who seek those titles for their own sake, as a way of setting themselves up among the community as more important. The Church would agree with this criticism. It would be wrong for our priests to use their position of authority to take advantage of us since their position of authority is given for the sake of service to the Church. In their position of leadership, priests serve as spiritual fathers to us, making sure we have all we need to grow in our faith. Through the ministry of priests, we are given access to new life in Christ and are nourished by the Word of God and the grace of the sacraments. So when we call our priests "father," we are recognizing the fact that, through the authority given by Christ, they share in God's work of guiding and sustaining our spiritual lives. They do not take the place of God. In fact, their job is to guide and support us as we grow in spiritual maturity as faithful children of our true Father in heaven.

SUGGESTED READING:

Matthew 23
Fulton Sheen, *A Priest is Not His Own*
Fr. Mario Romero, *Unabridged Christianity*
Alice Von Hildebrand, *Women and The Priesthood*

THINGS TO CONSIDER:

After an argument among the apostles about who was greatest among them Jesus said, "The kings of the Gentiles lord it over them and those in authority over them are addressed as 'Benefactors': but among you it shall not be so. Rather, let the greatest among you be as the youngest, and the leader as the servant" (Luke 22:25-26).

"Those who exercise authority should do so as a service" (CCC 2234).

"Whoever wishes to be great among you shall be your servant; whoever wishes to be first among you shall be your slave. Just so, the Son of Man did not come to be served but to serve and to give His life as a ransom for many" (Matthew 20:26-28).

SACRAMENTS

DO YOU HAVE TO BE BAPTIZED TO GO TO HEAVEN?

IN BRIEF:

Yes, if you believe Jesus and take Him at His word:

"Truly, truly, I say to you, unless one is born of water and the Spirit, he cannot enter the Kingdom of God."

- John 3:5

"He who believes and is baptized will be saved; but he who does not believe will be condemned."

- Mark 16:16

That being said, it's slightly more complicated than this, as there are instances of Baptism beyond the Sacrament of Baptism (with water). Read on.

IN DEPTH:

The New Testament is clear that Baptism in Christ is far different than the baptism offered by St. John the Baptist, and exceedingly efficacious. The grace of the sacrament does not just "clean" our exterior, but transforms and makes new our interior, erasing sins (including original sin) and their punishment (Acts 2:38, 22:16; Romans 6:3-4; Colossians 2:11-12).

The grace of the sacrament does not just "clean" our exterior, but transforms and makes new our interior, erasing sins (including original sin) and their punishment.

Our first Pope, St. Peter, also echoed the words of Christ, explaining the necessity of Baptism and the nature of what happens in a Biblical allusion to the salvation of Noah's family:

*"[...] who formerly did not obey, when God's patience waited in the days of Noah, during the building of the ark, in which a few, that is, eight persons, **were saved through water**. Baptism, which corresponds to this, now saves you, not as a removal of dirt from the body but as an appeal to God for a clear conscience, through the Resurrection of Jesus Christ."*

- 1 Peter 3:20-21, emphasis added

The Church has always held that among those souls "included" as saved – even if they had not been baptized with water – would be people who were martyred for Christ (baptism by blood). Included, too, are those who truly want to be Baptized but who – for whatever reason – are unable to receive the sacrament (baptism by desire). The Church is unwilling to say that unbaptized babies are or are not in heaven, but is quick to reaffirm that they are entrusted to the perfect mercy of God (*CCC* 1261).

There exists, too, the awareness that "not everyone" has had the opportunity to hear the Gospel or to make such a proclamation of faith. What about the tribesmen deep within the heart of the African or Australian continent who have never seen a television or heard a radio, for instance? What about a soul imprisoned in a communist country with no access to the Revelation of Jesus Christ? The Church acknowledges that in some extreme circumstances, these souls would need to hear of it before receiving it:

> *"The Lord Himself affirms that Baptism is necessary for salvation. He also commands His disciples to proclaim the Gospel to all nations and to baptize them. Baptism is necessary for salvation* **for those to whom the Gospel has been proclaimed and who have had the possibility of asking for this sacrament**. *The Church does not know of any means other than Baptism that assures entry into eternal beatitude [...]"*
> - *CCC* 1257, emphasis added

Note that this is not a "loophole" as much as it is a possible preclusion. As you read on in the paragraph, you'll note that the Church, again, reminds us that Baptism is the only assured way we know of for entry into heaven.

God is perfect mercy. Our Church, as the bride of Christ, desires all to know Christ and to be with Him for all eternity. It is with that in mind that the Church constantly reminds us of the magnitude of our apostolic calling, charged by Christ, Himself, in Matthew 28:28-20.

God is perfect mercy. Our Church, as the bride of Christ, desires all to know Christ and to be with Him for all eternity.

The Second Vatican Council, too, reaffirmed God's great mercy toward those to whom Baptism was never a true option, essentially saying that God offers *everyone* the opportunity for salvation, even if in unperceivable ways:

> *"All this holds true not only for Christians, but for all men of good will in whose hearts grace works in an unseen way. For, since Christ died for all men, and since the ultimate vocation of man is in fact one, and divine, we ought to believe that the Holy Spirit **in a manner known only to God offers to every man the possibility of being associated with this paschal mystery**."*
>
> — Gaudium et Spes, 22, emphasis added

It's important to note that this is not the Church saying Baptism is unnecessary – far from it. This is the Church celebrating the divine mercy and unfathomable mystery of God.

SUGGESTED READING:

CCC 1023, 1987, 1992, 2020, 2068, 2813
Pope Benedict XVI, *Introduction to Christianity*
Scott Hahn, *Swear to God: The Promise and Power of the Sacraments*

WHY DO CATHOLICS BAPTIZE INFANTS?

IN BRIEF:

The Catholic Church baptizes babies because they have a tendency to poop...a lot. They need all the baths they can get. There may be an even deeper, more catechetical response to this question, though. Let's take a look at that.

First, to be clear, there is not a single Biblical passage that would inhibit baptizing an infant. Second, the capacity to "reason" is not a prerequisite of Baptism; put simply, Baptism is not just about a child (or any person) "choosing" God as much as it is about God blessing that child with the gift of a new identity (divine Sonship). Thirdly, Baptism is more than a symbolic action and must be understood as such.

IN DEPTH:

God formed with Abraham the Old Covenant (and by extension, with his people); in it, circumcision was the sign of their covenant relationship with God. The circumcision was performed eight days after their birth (Genesis 17:12; Leviticus 12:3; Luke 1:59), which would clearly mean that the eight day old baby was not "choosing" a relationship with God out of their own, personal reason.

When Christ came and ushered in the New Covenant, Baptism replaced circumcision as the sign. Baptism accomplished what circumcision merely signified.

When Christ came and ushered in the New Covenant, Baptism replaced circumcision as the sign. Baptism accomplished what circumcision merely signified. In both the Old and New Covenants, parents made the decision on behalf of their child. Children could later confirm the decision on their own.

We see, too, the apostles baptizing whole households of people (which would include children) in the name of Christ:

> "And when she was baptized, **with her household** [...] "
> - Acts 16:15, emphasis added).

*"I did baptize **also the household** of Stephanas."*
- 1 Corinthians 1:16, emphasis added

*"And they said, 'Believe in the Lord Jesus, and you will be saved, you **and your household**.' And they spoke the word of the Lord to him and to all that were in his house. And he took them the same hour of the night, and washed their wounds, and he was baptized at once, **with all his family**."*
- Acts 16:31-33, emphasis added

Jesus also made it clear to His apostles that children are not to be kept away from Him:

"[Jesus] said to them, "Let the children come to me, do not hinder them; for to such belongs the Kingdom of God."
- Mark 10:14

Scripture reminds us that "children are a blessing from the Lord" (Psalms 127:3). They are a gift to the parents. The greatest gift a parent can, in turn, give their child is the gift of a relationship with God – their Creator, Father, Savior, Lord, and Lover. The word "religion" comes from an ancient word meaning "relationship," by the way. As the water is poured out over the child's head, the oil applied, and the candle lit, the door to heaven is opened wide for that beautiful soul – young or old – to encounter God in a new way, as a true Father (Mark 14:36; Romans 8:15; Galatians 4:6). It is a gift that lasts far beyond the ritual ceremony. Baptism is, quite literally, a gift that lasts for eternity.

The greatest gift a parent can, in turn, give their child is the gift of a relationship with God – their Creator, Father, Savior, Lord, and Lover.

If you haven't thanked God recently for the gift of your own Baptism, fall on your knees now and do so. There is no greater blessing in this world than to be invited to the next one and to be called a "child of God."

SUGGESTED READING:
CCC 403, 1231-33, 1250-52, 1282, 1290
Staff of Catholic Answers, *The Essential Catholic Survival Guide*

WHY CAN'T MY NON-CATHOLIC FRIENDS RECEIVE THE EUCHARIST?

IN BRIEF:

The Church saying that non-Catholics cannot receive the Eucharist is not saying that they are unworthy; this has nothing to do with their spiritual worth. What this does have to do with is their beliefs, and what they would be proclaiming if they were to receive the Eucharist.

If your friend is not Catholic (and thus, has not gone through "First Communion" classes), then they have not received the catechetical faith formation necessary to ensure that they understand what the Eucharist is, what we Catholics believe, or the deep significance of the sacrament. Even if your friend is an "on-fire" Christian, who is baptized, the Church (that is to say, the Roman Catholic Church and your local parish), has no way of being sure what exactly the person believes, unless they've had the chance to educate the person through formation about Catholic doctrines.

Again, this is not a condemnation or a judgment about another person's worth. Everyone needs to realize what happens when we go forward for Communion and receive the Body, Blood, Soul, and Divinity of our Lord and Savior, Jesus Christ. When a Catholic utters, "Amen" while receiving the Eucharist they are saying, "I believe with all my heart, all my mind, all my soul, and all my strength that this is the Lord Jesus Christ, completely and truly." If your friend agrees with that statement, get them signed up for R.C.I.A. immediately! If they do not, it's a great opportunity to invite them to pray with you at Mass (from the pew) and to have a much longer conversation afterward about how blessed you are to receive, and how blessed they could be, too.

IN DEPTH:

Catholics believe that the Eucharist is truly the divine Flesh and Blood of Jesus, not a mere piece of bread representing Him and not just a memorial symbol of Him, but *truly* Him. Non-Catholics do not believe this fact, and as a result, are missing out on experiencing this incomprehensible depth of divine intimacy.

The Eucharist is far more than a symbolic gesture that enhances our contemplative prayer life. It is nothing short of a physical encounter with God's grace, one that exceeds and transcends mere thought and weaves our bodies and souls ever more tightly together. On the most fundamental level, that is why non-Catholics who attend a Catholic Mass cannot receive. It is less about their "worthiness" and more about not putting them in a position to denounce their own beliefs.

The Eucharist is far more than a symbolic gesture that enhances our contemplative prayer life.

A person of another denomination can be the greatest Christian on earth, even a far greater Christian than many Catholics who go forward to receive, but if they utter that "Amen," they are saying much more than a word; they are swearing a belief and entering into a sacramental covenant with God, the Father Almighty. Allowing a non-Catholic to receive the Eucharist is either asking them to denounce their own beliefs or saying that you don't really believe in the Real Presence of Christ. Either way, it's not too good.

Receiving the Eucharist was (and still is) seen as an incredibly sacred thing in the Early Church, just read the words of St. Paul:

"The cup of blessing that we bless, is it not a participation in the blood of Christ? The bread that we break, is it not a participation in the body of Christ?"

- 1 Corinthians 10:16

A person of another denomination can be the greatest Christian on earth, even a far greater Christian than many Catholics who go forward to receive, but if they utter that "Amen," they are saying much more than a word.

"For I received from the Lord what I also handed on to you, that the Lord Jesus, on the night He was handed over, took bread, and, after He had given thanks, broke it and said, "This is my body that is for you. Do this in remembrance of me." In the same way also the cup, after supper, saying, "This cup is the new covenant in my blood. Do this, as often as you drink it, in remembrance of me." For as often as you eat this bread and drink the cup, you proclaim the death of the Lord until He comes. Therefore whoever eats the bread or drinks the cup of the Lord unworthily will have to answer for the body and blood of the Lord. A person should examine

himself, and so eat the bread and drink the cup. For anyone who eats and drinks without discerning the body, eats and drinks judgment on himself [...]"

- 1 Corinthians 11:23-29

Put simply, non-Catholics can't receive the Eucharist out of mutual respect. In addition, most Christians might be surprised to learn that the Bible says it is a no-no too (as seen above). St. Paul warned people about going forward to receive the true Flesh and Blood of Christ if they did not believe it to be so or were not in a state to do so. This warning also encompasses Catholics who are in a state of mortal sin who, prior to receiving Christ in His most precious Body and Blood, should get to Reconciliation.

Be sure that your friend knows they are always welcome, and not being able to receive the Eucharist does not mean they are "unworthy" as much as "unprepared" at this time. Invite them to make a "spiritual communion" with Christ rather than physically receiving.

St. Paul warned people about going forward to receive the true Flesh and Blood of Christ if they did not believe it to be so or were not in a state to do so.

It is good to invite friends from other religious backgrounds to join you for Mass. Be sure to take time prior to arriving to explain the ritual and the movements and postures they'll experience (i.e. standing, kneeling, singing and silence). Additionally, explain the restrictions on non-Catholics receiving before it's time to process forward for communion; it will spare both of you embarrassment or awkwardness. Most dioceses have guidelines for what non-Catholics can do and pray during Communion. We always want to make people of other denominations feel welcome, but never at the expense of our own Church. We are Catholic, and we are proud of it.

SUGGESTED READING:
CCC 1398, 1374, 1322, 1212, 790, 1003
Cardinal Joseph Ratzinger (Pope Benedict XVI), *God Is Near Us: The Eucharist, the Heart of Life*
Fr. Robert Barron, *Eucharist*
Scott Hahn, *The Lamb's Suppers*

HOW DO WE KNOW THE EARLY CHRISTIANS BELIEVED IN THE TRUE PRESENCE OF CHRIST IN THE EUCHARIST?

IN BRIEF:
We know they believed in the True Presence because they refused to leave right after Communion, like so many modern "believers" do. Just kidding.

Scripturally speaking, it is clear that the apostles took Christ at His word. First, they handed on to the early Church the Sacramental fullness of what Christ had handed on to them, most notably St. Paul (1 Corinthians 10:16, 11:23-29). St. Paul's entire basis for his teachings on what is and is not acceptable within the liturgy (in the aforementioned readings from 1 Corinthians) was a result of the Tradition and theology he had received, witnessed, and abided by through the direction of the Holy Spirit and the instruction of the other apostles.

St. Paul undoubtedly believed in the True Presence of the Eucharist, and he wasn't even present in the room at the Last Supper. This fact further validates the truth of the oral tradition, apostolic teaching, and the ongoing formation of "new" Christians in the early Church.

IN DEPTH:
Following the Resurrection and the Ascension, several practices changed, most notably the day and form of worship. The New Testament offers tangible examples to how the "culture" of worship in the early Church changed, noting that the breaking of the bread and communal life shifted to the first day of the week (Acts 2:42, 20:7; 1 Corinthians 16:2). They didn't "go back" to how they'd worshipped in the past. This form of Sabbath worship (on the first day and not the seventh) was new for the Christians.

Almost overnight thousands of people abandoned their practice of worshipping on Saturday and moved their Sabbath worship to Sunday to commemorate Christ's Resurrection. What they did within their worship, too, brought a new fulfillment to age-old prayers and rituals. As we see in the passage from Acts, just following the Spirit's descent at Pentecost, the first Christians' formation came from the apostles and no longer just the Torah. Additionally, the Eucharist played an integral role in their worship:

> *"And they devoted themselves to the apostles' teaching and fellowship, **to the breaking of bread** and the prayers."*
>
> - Acts 2:42, emphasis added

St. Paul wasn't the only one who understood the Eucharist to be the literal body and blood and more than a symbolic, memorial meal. St. Peter echoes the words of Christ and bids us out into the deep when he tell us:

The New Testament offers tangible examples to how the "culture" of worship in the early Church changed, noting that the breaking of the bread and communal life shifted to the first day of the week.

> *"He has granted to us His precious and very great promises, that through these you may escape from the corruption that is in the world because of passion, and become partakers of the **divine nature.**"*
>
> - 2 Peter 1:4, emphasis added

When we partake (take part) in the Eucharist we are not merely eating bread or drinking wine. As Christ promised, we are eating His very Flesh and Blood. We are "abiding" in Him (John 15:4-6; 1 John 2:27-28, 4:13) in the most tangible way when we receive the Eucharistic Lord.

Through the Eucharist, we receive the grace of God in a practical way. Grace can be described as "God's life in us." It's interesting to note that the Greek word St. Paul uses for **grace** is *charis*, which you might recognize from the word *Eucharist*. It's through the *Eucharist* that God most physically places His grace within us.

When we partake (take part) in the Eucharist we are not merely eating bread or drinking wine. As Christ promised, we are eating His very flesh and blood.

Beyond these Scriptural realities, there are dozens of writings from the saints and early Church Fathers during the dawn of Christianity all consistently proclaiming the early Christian belief and understanding of Christ's true Eucharistic presence. These writings not only demonstrate personal assurance but the even larger cultural understanding and practices for centuries after the Last Supper.

Read through a few for yourself:

> *"I have no taste for corruptible food nor for the pleasures of this life. I desire the Bread of God, which is the Flesh of Jesus Christ, who was the seed of David; and for drink I desire His Blood, which is love incorruptible."*
>> - St. Ignatius of Antioch in his *Letter to the Smyrnaeans*

> *"We call this food Eucharist; and no one is permitted to partake of it, except one who believes our teaching to be true[...] for not as common bread nor common drink do we receive these; but since Jesus Christ our Savior was made incarnate by the word of God and had both flesh and blood for our salvation, so too, as we have been taught, the food which has been made into the Eucharist by the Eucharistic prayer set down by Him, and by the change of which our blood and flesh is nourished, is both the Flesh and the Blood of that incarnated Jesus."*
>> - St. Justin Martyr in his *First Apology*

We call this food Eucharist; and no one is permitted to partake of it, except one who believes our teaching to be true.

> *"He [Jesus] has declared the cup, a part of creation, to be His own Blood, from which He causes our blood to flow; and the bread, a part of creation. He has established as His own Body, from which He gives increase to our bodies."*
>> - St. Irenaeus in his writing *Against Heresies*

> *"He [Jesus] Himself, therefore, having declared and said of the Bread, "This is My Body," who will dare any longer to doubt? And when He Himself has affirmed and said, 'This is My Blood,' who can ever hesitate and say it is not His Blood? Do not, therefore, regard the bread and wine as simply that, for they are, according to the Master's declaration, the Body and Blood of Christ. Even though the senses suggest to you the other, let faith make you firm. Do not judge in this matter by taste, but be fully assured by faith, not doubting that you have been deemed worthy of the Body and Blood of Christ."*
>> - St. Cyril of Jerusalem

> *"Take note of those who held heterodox opinions on the grace of Jesus Christ which has come to us, and see how contrary their opinions are to the mind of God. They abstain from the Eucharist*

and from prayer, because they do not confess that the Eucharist is the Flesh of our Savior Jesus Christ, Flesh which suffered for our sins and which the Father, in His goodness, raised up again."

- St. Ignatius of Antioch in his *Letter to the Romans*

SUGGESTED READING:

CCC 1373-77

Cardinal Joseph Ratzinger (Pope Benedict XVI), *God Is Near Us: The Eucharist, the Heart of Life*

Fr. Robert Barron, *Eucharist*

Fr. Mario Romero, *Unabridged Christianity*

Scott Hahn, *The Lamb's Supper*

ISN'T EATING THE BODY AND BLOOD OF CHRIST CANNIBALISM?

IN BRIEF:

If someone hears you're Catholic and tells you that – by extension – you are a cannibal, there is only one acceptable response:

When they say you're a "cannibal" get a crazed, starved look in your eye and then begin staring at their arm. Lick your lips like you haven't eaten in weeks and continue staring at their arm, then look back with the straightest face ever and reply, "Well, yes, maybe I am...I'm quite hungry and your arm looks delicious."

Okay, do not do that.

And for anyone who thinks the above idea is inappropriate – it was a joke, with absolutely no seriousness behind it - just an innocent joke. If you're still insulted, check under the sofa cushions for your sense of humor. Just kidding, again...or am I?

Life's too short not to laugh. It's also too short not to experience the true, living, and active God of all creation in the simplest of His creation, ordinary bread and wine, which through the power of the Holy Spirit, the Spirit of Love, are transubstantiated into the extraordinary, grace-filled blessing that He gave us as Eucharist.

The assertion that a Catholic is a cannibal is so absurd, it almost doesn't deserve a response. But, since we're here, let's answer it anyway.

IN DEPTH:

The Roman Catholic Church maintains that the Eucharist is truly the Body, Blood, Soul, and Divinity of Jesus Christ (CCC 1373-1381). We discuss this a little further on page 128.

Notice that I said maintains and not merely "teaches" because the True Presence of Christ in the Eucharist was understood and handed on since immediately after Christ's self-gift in the Upper Room at the Last Supper, and it has been maintained ever since by the Church.

The above truth means that we absolutely believe it is Christ's Body and Blood, in divine form, which we do consume.

Cannibalism is a very different thing. A cannibal is someone who eats human flesh and blood, and through that, eats all that goes along with it, like muscles and tissues and veins or organs or whatever else. It's important to note, too, that a cannibal kills his victim, but Jesus is not killed when we receive communion.

We absolutely believe it is Christ's Body and Blood, in Divine form, which we do consume.

As a Catholic, you are eating Christ's Divine Flesh and Blood. The Eucharist is the Body and Blood of the risen, glorified Jesus in His risen and glorified state, just as St. John explains to all of us in the Gospel (John 6:53-55). That passage from the Gospel of John also reminds us that it was Christ, Himself, who encouraged and, later, commanded that we eat His Flesh and drink His Blood (Matthew 26:26-28). This act was neither homicidal nor suicidal. Christ offers us His glorified self to nourish and transform us by His grace. We also do not believe that the Eucharist is a mere symbol or that Christ was speaking symbolically, which you can read more about on page 134.

The Eucharist is the Body and Blood of the risen, glorified Jesus in His risen and glorified state, just as St. John explains to all of us in the Gospel (John 6:53-55).

SUGGESTED READING:
CCC 1373-81
The Staff of Catholic Answers, *The Essential Catholic Survival Guide*

HOW DO WE KNOW THAT JESUS WAS SPEAKING LITERALLY WHEN HE SAID, "THIS IS MY BODY?"

IN BRIEF:

The full question usually goes something like this:

"While the Bible has Jesus saying, 'This is my body,' it also has Him saying He is 'the door' and 'the vine,' so, how can we, as Catholics, be sure Jesus was talking about His Real and actual Presence in the Eucharist and not just a metaphor like when He said 'I am the door' (John 10:9) or 'I am the vine' (John 15:5)?"

Perhaps you've heard someone say, "It's raining cats and dogs outside," but when you looked, there were no felines or canines falling from the sky. Maybe you've heard someone say, "I'm dead tired," but the person still had a pulse. You get the idea. Some phrases are just figures of speech, idioms that imply a meaning but are not to be taken literally. Some Christians assert that is what Jesus meant during the Last Supper and point to these other "door" and "vine" allusions to back up their claim. What many well-intentioned brothers and sisters in Christ fail to understand is that you must take the Gospels as a whole to properly understand Jesus' teaching, not one or two verses out of context.

Elsewhere in the Gospels, Jesus speaks about food in a symbolic way (John 4:31-34; Matthew 16:5-12), but when the disciples take Him literally, He explains that He is speaking figuratively. Now, contrast those episodes with what happens in John chapter six (specifically John 6:51-56), and you'll see that Jesus does nothing to dissuade the literal interpretation (not the symbolic); Jesus even empowers it and re-affirms it! This clear teaching in John 6 only further strengthens the literal nature of Christ's words in the Upper Room (Matthew 26:26; Mark 14:22; Luke 22:19), and St. Paul's forceful teaching on the reality of Christ's True Presence in the Eucharist (1 Corinthians 11:24).

IN DEPTH:

Hopefully, through the example above, you can see how context is so important. Many Christians understand the content of Scripture (the details within it) but the **context** is even more important because it shows how all those details go together ("context" literally means woven together).

While it's true that Jesus used figures of speech and metaphors to explain the heavenly mystery to people, there is a difference in context between when He said, "I am the door" or "I am the vine" and when He said, "I am the Bread of Life" (John 6:35). Breaking open the "In Brief" section a little further, just look at what happened right after He said it: people were confused (John 6:42), people grew angry (John 6:52), and people even began to walk away (John 6:66).

The fact is, however, that He didn't correct what He said. No, He said it even louder, and said it again and again and again:

> *"Amen, amen, I say to you, unless you eat the flesh of the Son of Man and drink His blood, you do not have life within you. Whoever eats my flesh and drinks my blood has eternal life, and I will raise Him on the last day. For my flesh is true food, and my blood is true drink."*
>
> - John 6:53-55

Ask yourself, why didn't Jesus correct their misunderstanding? He was ministering; He wanted people to hear God's truth, and He was building a large following. He would have to be crazy to let them go simply because they 'misunderstood' His metaphor. In other cases, when people were confused, Jesus was sure to "clarify" what He was saying (Matthew 16:5-12, for instance). Also, He would have a moral obligation to explain what He "really" meant to them; their salvation was at stake if they abandoned their former religious beliefs for Him!

Now, since we weren't present when He spoke these words, we have to rely on the Scriptures. One of the beautiful gifts of being Catholic is that we hold both Sacred Scripture and Sacred Tradition in equal esteem, very different but both very important. The Magisterium (the teaching authority of the Church) is invaluable in this way, helping us to sift through all the different references, languages, and translations and unearthing the intended meaning.

Some may try to tell you that the Church "edited" or "bent" Christ's words and teachings to prove their own doctrines, but that accusation is quickly disproved by St. Paul. Remember, St. Paul wasn't in the Upper Room during the Last Supper, but it is astoundingly clear in his letter to the Corinthians that he believes and proclaims the Real Presence in the Eucharist:

Some may try to tell you that the Church "edited" or "bent" Christ's words and teachings to prove their own doctrines, but that accusation is quickly disproved by St. Paul.

"The cup of blessing that we bless, is it not a participation in the Blood of Christ? The bread that we break, is it not a participation in the Body of Christ?"
- 1 Corinthians 10:16

"Therefore whoever eats the bread or drinks the cup of the Lord unworthily will have to answer for the Body and Blood of the Lord. For anyone who eats and drinks without discerning the body, eats, and drinks judgment on himself"
- 1 Corinthians 11:27,29

Why would St. Paul say that? That's right...Tradition.

Through the handing on of Sacred Tradition and studying the works of our early Church Fathers, including the epistles of St. Paul, we come to find out where the emphasis in certain Scriptures must have been placed by Christ, Himself. There were eyewitness groups of His followers doing as they had seen and been taught, by God (Christ) Himself. That is Sacred Tradition: the handing on of the faith and the practices of faith, instituted by Christ.

It's important to note that there are principally two "ways" of reading Scripture or two "senses": the literal and the spiritual. The spiritual sense, however, must be broken down even further because it is seemingly more abstract. There are three more ways of interpreting Scripture spiritually, whether it is allegorical, moral, or anagogical. Allegories teach truth in a symbolic way. Moral interpretations demonstrate how these truths are applied and lived out in our daily lives. Anagogy points us to our ultimate end and destiny.

When we study a passage of Scripture we look, first, to the literal meaning, asking what the Holy Spirit is trying to convey through the author using figures of speech, cultural references, allusions to history, and literal events. There might also be spiritual meanings in addition to the literal meaning. It is vital to examine each of these – with the help of the Church (who prayerfully compiled and preserved the Scriptures) — for an accurate study.

For instance, Jesus literally healed the man born blind. That was a historical moment and a literal truth. That healing also had allegorical, moral, and anagogical elements to it. Allegorically it signifies Baptism, how we are all born into the blindness of original sin and how the water (Christ's spit) washes away our blindness and makes us new (Baptism). Morally, it encourages us to seek Christ in our sin and in our infirmities, seeking our healing in His grace. Anagogically, it reminds us that we will be made new in heaven one day.

> There were eyewitness groups of His followers doing as they had seen and been taught, by God (Christ) Himself. That is Sacred Tradition: the handing on of the faith and the practices of faith, instituted by Christ.

Quite obviously, there are many different things being achieved through one passage or one story. Be thankful for the Holy Spirit, so present in the teaching authority of the Church, guiding us to go ever deeper into what the Scriptures meant to our ancestors then and to us today.

SUGGESTED READING:
CCC 1373-81
Mark Shea, *Making Senses of Scripture*
Dave Armstrong, *The Catholic Verses*
Frank Sheed, *Theology for Beginners*

WHAT DOES IT MEAN TO SAY THAT JESUS IS THE "LAMB OF GOD"?

IN BRIEF:

"Lamb of God" is one of the most common titles associated with Christ. We hear it in hymns and other songs and see it in murals and paintings, on icons and stained glass. It is the first title uttered by St. John the Baptist as our Lord approached the Jordan River (John 1:29). In that famous utterance, the Baptist gives us a little insight into not only the meaning, but also Christ's purpose:

> "The next day he saw Jesus coming toward him, and said, "Behold, the Lamb of God, **who takes away the sin of the world**!"
>
> - John 1:29, emphasis added

Upon hearing that verse many people may be confused, however, as to how a lamb can take away sins (which we'll deal with in the "In Dtepth" section). Christ's title as the "Lamb of God" points us not only to His mission but also to His identity.

Sacrifice is one of our most basic human actions and needs. In sacrificing something to God, we reaffirm who He is and who we are not; we demonstrate that God is greater than we are and that all good gifts come from Him. Since everything we have is ultimately a gift from God (except sin – that's all ours), we honor God and remind ourselves who God really is by offering our gifts back to Him through a sacrifice.

Once our relationship with God was darkened by sin, the need for sacrifice grew stronger. As our sins grew, God even called for a bloody sacrifice, killing an animal in reparation for our sins. The blood was holy because it was seen as the source of life. No animal sacrifice could cover the greatness of our sin, however; our debt was too large and our sin too great, until God took flesh (the Incarnation) and did what we could never do by ourselves: He came to save us. Jesus is the one who not only paid our debt of sin but who conquered sin and death once and for all (Romans 6:23, 1 Corinthians 15:21).

IN DEPTH:

To better understand Scripture and our salvation history, it is helpful to view the stories of the Bible – both within the Old and New Testaments – through the lens of a *covenant* (as we briefly discussed on page 11).

A covenant is a sacred, familial bond between God and man and/or between people. It is far more than a contract. A covenant is more than doing mutually beneficial favors or an exchange of goods and services; a covenant is an exchange of self. When God enters into a covenant with Adam and Eve, He is offering all of Himself to them and inviting Adam and Eve to offer themselves back to Him in return. After our first parents broke their end of the covenant through sin, there

> **When God enters into a covenant with Adam and Eve, He is offering all of Himself to them and inviting Adam and Eve to offer themselves back to Him in return.**

was a debt to be paid. God held up His end of the covenant, but we broke ours. Shortly thereafter, Cain's displeasing sacrifice to God (Genesis 4) and murder of his brother Abel, things went from bad to worse. As time went on, God formed new covenants with Noah, with Abraham, with Moses, and with David - all of which were broken, as well.

The problem is that God's holiness demands justice. Since God is perfect Justice and perfect Love, He cannot just dismiss the covenant promise and consequence; if He did, He wouldn't fulfill His word and that violates the very nature of God. On the other hand, He loved us too much to let us just die. God could not just dismiss the sin, but God also did not want to just dismiss us. We were left with a problem that only God could solve...and in Christ Jesus, He did what we couldn't do. Jesus was the answer to our sinful past and our hopeless future.

> **Since God is perfect Justice and perfect Love, He cannot just dismiss the covenant promise and consequence; if He did, He wouldn't fulfill His word and that violates the very nature of God.**

During the tenth plague in Exodus, God prescribed a way for His people to be protected from death. He ordered every household to select a lamb, to slaughter it, eat its flesh, and cover the wooden doorpost of their home with the lamb's blood. You can read about this, in detail, in Exodus chapter twelve. The night the angel of death passed over the land of Egypt (yes, that's where we get the term "Passover") and in any home without the blood of the lamb upon its door, the firstborn male child died, including animals (Exodus 12:29).

Not long after the Passover, the iniquities and sins of God's children grew stronger, escalating with the worship of a golden calf (Exodus 32). It was at that time that God commanded animal sacrifices in atonement for their sins. It's important to note here that animal sacrifice was quite commonplace in the ancient world, so God was using a well-known practice but reorienting it to Him (rather than to false Gods). In fact, the animals God commanded the Hebrews to sacrifice were actually Gods to other people, further making God's point regarding His status as the one, true God. In commanding His people to spill these animals' blood and then eat them, God made the gravest sin for the Egyptians (in this case) the path to forgiveness for His children (the Israelites). God had taken the Israelites out of Egypt, but in calling for this bloody sacrifice God was trying to "take Egypt out of the Israelites."

In Leviticus chapter sixteen, God told Moses and Aaron to select two goats for a sacrificial offering to atone for (atone means to reconcile or "make amends for") the sins of the people. The first goat was to be killed and his blood was to be sprinkled on what was called the "Mercy Seat" on the Ark of the Covenant (which held the Ten Commandments). When God saw the blood of the offering, He would remain merciful to His sinful children and His forgiveness would be poured out upon them as they ate the animal's flesh. They were now in "communion" with the animal who had taken their place and paid their debt.

The priest would then lay hands on the second goat and confer the sins of the people on it. This goat (known as the scapegoat) would be allowed to live but would bear the sins of the people. He would be taken far into the wilderness and set free and God would "remember their sins no more" (Isaiah 1:18).

Fast forward hundreds of years and you find Jesus gathering His apostles for the Last Supper on the Feast of Passover, which commemorated the aforementioned events of Exodus twelve. At that meal, Christ spoke of a new covenant:

"Now as they were eating, Jesus took bread, and blessed, and broke it, and gave it to the disciples and said, "Take, eat; this is my

body." And He took a cup, and when He had given thanks He gave it to them, saying, "Drink of it, all of you; for this is my blood of the covenant, which is poured out for many for the forgiveness of sins"
- Matthew 26:26-28

Here we see Christ – as the Lamb of God – offering us His flesh to eat in the Upper Room on Holy Thursday night, when the apostles entered into communion with Him in an extraordinary new way. Each time we go to Mass, we are participating in Christ's once-and-for-all sacrifice 2000 years ago. The blood He shed on the cross (like the lamb's blood on the doorpost) saves us from death, and the Flesh and Blood we consume renews our covenant (but a new, eternal covenant) with Him.

Each time we go to Mass, we are participating in Christ's once-and-for-all sacrifice 2000 years ago.

At the original Passover, the Israelites were set free from the chains of slavery. Through the sacraments, still today, we are set free from sin and death and offered new life.

Obviously, the title "Lamb of God" carries with it great Biblical history and significance. This is yet another example of how the Old Testament points to Jesus and how in Christ (and in the New Testament) the Old Testament takes on all-new meaning.

SUGGESTED READING:
CCC 1322-1419
Scott Hahn, *The Lamb's Supper*
Scott Hahn, *A Father Who Keeps His Promises*
Thomas Nash, *Worthy is the Lamb*
Fulton Sheen, *A Priest Is Not His Own*

WHAT IS TRANSUBSTANTIATION EXACTLY?

IN BRIEF:

We Catholics love big words: epiclesis, doxology, catechesis, Magisterium. Perhaps no word is more important and more misunderstood than transubstantiation.

Transubstantiation is the term used to describe what literally happens at every Catholic Mass, through the power of the Holy Spirit working through the sacramental priesthood of Jesus Christ. Transubstantiation is when the gifts of bread and wine are *substantially* changed into the real flesh and blood of Jesus Christ; it is the substance that is changed, not the form, meaning that it will look the same (in form) but on a "deeper" level (substance), it is different. This is why the term is transubstantiated not "transformed." At the Council of Trent, the Catholic Church summarized transubstantiation quite nicely. To read more about it, check out your *Catechism* (*CCC* 1376-77).

IN DEPTH:

Many Christians (and some Catholics unfortunately) have a difficult time with this teaching because it does not "appear" that the bread and wine change. How do we, as Catholics, explain our belief in the Real Presence, if the bread and the wine still look like simple bread and wine? Think about it: it would be a lot easier if all of a sudden the bread oozed blood, or if we used clear glasses, and white wine turned into red wine, right?

Well, it's complicated to explain in a small amount of space, but let's give it a try.

There are two "levels" that make up an object: the accidents and the substance. The accidents are the appearance, taste, look, and feel of an object, but the substance is what it really is. Take a chair; it has accidents and it has a substance. The accidents of the chair are four legs, a seat, a back – some wood and some screws. The substance of the chair is comprised of wood molecules that have been fashioned into the form of a chair.

Say that you saw the chair in several pieces, and then you took those pieces of wood and reconfigured them with nails to make a coffee table. You've changed the *accidents* of the chair into a table, but the substance of the chair has not been changed; it's still made up of wood molecules. Make sense?

If the accidents changed it would be trans*form*ation. Since it is not the accidents, but rather the substance that changes in Mass, it is trans*substantia*tion. So, at Mass the *accidents* of the bread and wine do not change – it will have the same color, size, smell, and taste and will still look like bread wafers and regular wine - but through the power of the Holy Spirit, the *substance* of the bread and wine are altered into Christ's Body and Blood on the altar.

The Eucharist is not a mystery to be solved, but a mystery to behold. The gifts are not transformed but *transubstantiated*. This miracle turns you into a walking tabernacle, literally changing you from the inside out. This uniquely intimate expression of God's grace, through Holy Communion, has a power to change us like nothing else on earth.

SUGGESTED READING:
CCC 1373-1377, 1404, 1413
The Staff of Catholic Answers, *The Essential Catholic Survival Guide*
Dave Armstrong, *The Catholic Verses*
Frank Sheed, *Theology for Beginners*

WHY GO TO ANOTHER SINNER FOR CONFESSION IF ONLY GOD CAN FORGIVE SINS?

IN BRIEF:

Say that you work at a gas station, and a car pulls in for directions. Now when the driver gets out, how do you know what directions to give them? How do you know whether to tell them that they're on the right road or the wrong road? Do you just *guess* based on looking at them, or do you *listen* to them first?

It's the same way with a priest during confession. Christ gave His apostles – as part of their new priesthood – the ability to "bind" or to "loose" sins, basically to forgive them in His Name.

Jesus said, "Peace be with you. As the Father has sent me, so I send you." And when He had said this, He breathed on them and said to them, "Receive the Holy Spirit. Whose sins you forgive are forgiven them, and whose sins you retain are retained" (John 20:21-23).

By necessity, a priest can only know whether to forgive sins or hold them bound *once he has heard them* — hearing the sins is essential.

While you might be thinking to yourself, "But doesn't God already know my sins? Why do I have to admit them out loud to a priestly representative?" The question you must ask is "why" Christ did what He did and said what He said in the episode from the Scripture passage above? God does not do anything by accident. Jesus is intentional. The Scriptures, too, only contain the inspired words of God, free of anything unnecessary. So God must have had a purpose when He gave us this truth.

IN DEPTH:

Remember, the Church doesn't just "make things up" to keep priests busy or keep people in line. When we discuss Confession through the Sacrament of Reconciliation, we are taking Christ at His word (just as we do with the Eucharist). Notice, too, what Christ did when He empowered His apostles with this charge... God breathed on them. This was more than a polite gesture or revelation of divinely good breath. God's breath holds the power of life and animation as we saw in the garden of Eden (Genesis 2:7); why would the Spirit inspire those words through St. John if that detail was not incredibly important? Through the breath of Christ, the Spirit is unleashed and the power given to breathe similar peace upon all.

Christ gives us the sacraments. For over 2000 years, Jesus' command "to bind and to loose" has been passed down from apostle to apostle; our bishops are the inheritors of their authority. At ordination, priests get their ability to perform the sacraments from their bishop. Therefore they must forgive sin in Christ's Name. St. Paul reminded us, too, that the apostles were Christ's ambassadors of **Reconciliation** (check out 2 Corinthians 5:17-20), after all.

It's essential to remember, too, that there is no such thing as a private sin. Whether we have committed the sin by ourselves or with other people, a sin always has effects throughout the entire community of the faith. Let's explore that on two levels:

• Sin changes the way we interact with other people. Maybe because of the shame or guilt of the sin or maybe because of fear of being found out, sin affects our behavior.

• St. Paul's analogy of the Body of Christ (Romans 12:3-8) states that all believers in Christ are united. This means that when one of us sins, we damage the greater Body that all of us belong to. Therefore, Reconciliation must be done through a representative of the Body, and in the Catholic Church – founded by Christ and empowered by the Holy Spirit – we call that representative "Father" (which you can read more about on page 114).

Most importantly, though, we must remember that *it is Jesus who forgives our sins*. It is Jesus who died so that our sins would be forgiven, that we would be able to join Him in heaven. We aren't going "to" the priest as much as we are going "through" the priest. We're going to God directly as well as through the priestly ministry ordained in His Name and for His purpose. Jesus entrusted His Church on earth to sinners – partly because we're all He had to choose from. He also empowered His Church with the Holy Spirit. It is Jesus who died so that our sins would be forgiven, that we would be able to join Him in heaven.

In **James 5:14-16** you'll notice that the sins of the sick are forgiven through the Sacrament of Anointing, but notice who has to be called in order for that to happen:

> *"Is any among you sick? Let him call for the elders of the church, and let them pray over him, anointing him with oil in the name of the Lord; and the prayer of faith will save the sick man, and the Lord will raise him up; **and if he has committed sins, he will be forgiven**. Therefore confess your sins to one another, and pray for one another, that you may be healed. The prayer of a righteous man has great power in its effects."*
>
> - James 4:14-16, emphasis added

In this passage the "elders" referred to were the presbyters – the priests! Obviously just "anyone" could not do this.

It is Jesus who died so that our sins would be forgiven, that we would be able to join Him in heaven. We aren't going "to" the priest as much as we are going "through" the priest. We're going to God directly as well as through the priestly ministry ordained in His Name and for His purpose.

In the Sacrament of Reconciliation, the priest is sitting in the name of Christ. At the end of Reconciliation when the priest says, "... I absolve you," he is speaking in *"persona Christi Capitis,"* which means he is sitting there "in the person of Christ." It is a great reminder to us as he says, " I absolve you" rather than "Jesus absolves you."

Some Christians assert, "I can just have a personal relationship with God, and He will forgive my sins" which is problematic on a few different levels we'll explore.

- Some people keep it all inside. There are just too many people – even Christians - walking around feeling guilty all the time. Many dislike the idea of the kind of humility it necessitates to share their sin with another. As James 4:16 reminds us (above), we're supposed to share our sins with other believers, even if that makes us vulnerable.

- Some people share with friends. One popular trend with our Protestant brothers and sisters is having an accountability partner. An accountability partner is a friend that you can trust and confide in, sharing those times when sinned and then giving advice and support. If nothing else, having an accountability partner is convicting because you know that you'll have to tell a friend when you've sinned, and thus you try to avoid sin to save the embarrassment. Having an "accountability partner" sounds a lot like going to Confession but without the grace of absolution.

• Some people share with counselors. Counseling is great and can tremendously bless a soul. Priests hear confessions all the time and are trained in counseling, too — helping people resolve issues that lead to grave sin. A priest can give insightful advice and spiritual direction that even a counselor may not be able to, and again, a priest offers Christ's absolution.

Confession offers us Christ's grace and mercy, the chance to grow in humility, the assurance of forgiveness, spiritual counsel and the alleviation of our own failed attempts to justify our sins; who wouldn't want to take part in such a gift from God? Thank Jesus for such an amazing gift!

As E. W. Lutzer put it, "Forgiveness is always free, but that doesn't mean that Confession is always easy."

SUGGESTED READING:
CCC 1446, 1461-66, 1491
Scott Hahn, *Lord Have Mercy: The Healing Power of Confession*
Life Teen, *Come Clean*

SIN AND SALVATION

WHAT IS SIN? WHAT IS ORIGINAL SIN?

IN BRIEF:

Sin is an offense against God because it is a misuse of the freedom granted to us for the purpose of freely accepting the gift of life that He wants to share with us. Sin affects our relationship with God and our neighbor, and it damages our very ability to love and grow in holiness. Through the disobedience of Adam and Eve, all mankind lost access to the grace of sharing in God's own life, and so are *spiritually dead* and in need of salvation. This state of being without grace and divine life is referred to as the state of *original sin*.

IN DEPTH:

Sin is one of those things that most might generally understand but would probably have trouble defining or explaining. If you have grown up around Christianity at all, you most likely think of sin as "doing what is wrong or bad" or "not following what God wants us to do." Now there is nothing really wrong with these understandings. Sin certainly is doing something bad and contrary to what God wants us to do, but there is really so much more to it. When we look more closely at what sin actually is, we will better understand what is so *bad* about it and *why* God doesn't want us to do it.

We have to remember that God made us to share in His divine life, to experience the love and goodness of the Trinity. That is the goal and purpose of our lives, which means that everything we do should move us in that direction. But there is a catch: God has given us free will. He doesn't force His love upon us, but extends an invitation to us to enter into a relationship with Him. God has given us freedom, but too often we tend to think of freedom as the ability to do whatever we want. Especially in our modern society, freedom is usually understood as free reign to do anything; we can wrongly think that freedom means there is no one telling us what to do.

When we understand freedom this way, we tend to see our faith as full of rules and restrictions, and about what we *aren't* allowed to do. But this is a complete misunderstanding of what freedom actually is. We were given our freedom so that we could *freely accept* God's invitation to know and love Him. This means that our freedom is only ever rightly exercised if it is used to freely embrace what is good and true.

God's laws and commandments are not given to us because God wants to make us miserable. They are given as a way of protecting us from using our freedom to lead us in the wrong direction. God tells us what to do and not do because He wants to help us use our free will in a way that will move us closer to Him. It's like an instruction manual for assembling a bike. I am free to follow or not follow the directions as I put together the bike, but either way the *purpose* of the instructions is not to restrict my freedom, but to guide me in the right assembly of the bike. When we follow the instructions, we know that we are moving in the right direction. It is the same with God's law. He gives us commandments and rules not to restrict our freedom, but to help us use our freedom the way it was meant to be used – to freely seek what is good.

So what does this have to do with sin? Well, sin is a *disordered* use of our freedom. When we sin we use our freedom in a way that it was never meant to be used. Understanding this helps us begin to see what is so bad about sin. It's not bad just because God says so; sin is bad because it involves using our freedom (the freedom that was given to enable us to know and love God) in ways that lead us away from the very purpose of our lives.

Related to this idea of sin being a misuse of our freedom and hindering our ability to achieve the goal of our lives is the fact that sin *wounds charity*. Now, unfortunately when most people hear the word charity, they think of giving money to the poor or working at a soup kitchen. Now these are certainly good things to do and things that are called for by the Gospel, but when we talk about charity here, we are talking about the *virtue* of charity (*caritas* in Latin), which is our very ability to love.

This virtue of charity (along with faith and love) is given to us as a supernatural gift by God to enable us to live and grow in holiness as children of God. In fact, the *Catechism of the Catholic Church* calls charity the "vital principle" within us (*CCC* 1856). Like the engine of a car, which enables the rest of the car to do what it was meant to do, charity is the driving force in us that enables us to live as God calls us to live. So when the Church says that sin "wounds charity," what this means is that sin damages our very ability to love. Sin attacks and damages the very thing within us that is meant to lead us closer to God. Like a car whose engine is damaged if driven improperly, sin hinders our ability to love God and others as we should by damaging the very source of love that God placed within us. As we saw before, when we understand sin in this way, we begin to see more clearly what is so bad about it. Sin is bad because it hinders our ability to live as His children and remain in His friendship.

Now, what about *original sin*? To understand original sin we need to look at the first four chapters of Genesis. When God created Adam and Eve, He placed them in a garden and told them that all of the trees in the garden were theirs to eat from... all but one. God commanded them not to eat from the *Tree of Knowledge of Good and Evil* and warned them that if they did eat from it, they would be doomed to die. They were free to eat from all the rest, but the Tree of Knowledge was off limits. Now, among the trees in the garden (the ones from which they were allowed to eat) was the *Tree of Life*, which is a symbol of the eternal life that God wanted to share with them. It is important to realize that Adam and Eve had free access to this tree. All they had to do was obey God's one command and all would be good.

Everything was going great until the serpent came along and tried to convince Eve that she wouldn't die if she ate from the *Tree of Knowledge of Good and Evil*. Now look at what the Bible says about Eve as she contemplated her decision; it says that she "saw that the tree was good for food, pleasing to the eye, and desirable for gaining wisdom" (Genesis 3:6). The fact that Eve considered the "goodness" of the forbidden fruit *before* eating it is worth noticing. Although we don't know exactly what more went through her mind, Eve could have easily looked at the tree and thought, *this is a good tree*, and *perhaps* she began to think to herself, *God doesn't want me to eat from this tree, maybe God doesn't want good things for me*. She also could have concluded from all of this that, *God doesn't love me; God wants to keep me from good things*. As we said earlier, we have a tendency to think that God's laws are meant to keep us from being happy, that God wants to spoil our fun because sin, at times, appears to be "good." And so we begin to doubt (whether consciously or sub-consciously) that God's commands are actually the best for us. What God was asking of Adam and Eve was trust — trust in His goodness and in His care for them. But instead of trusting in God, they disobeyed and misused their freedom.

So Adam and Eve sinned; then what? Well, remember the warning that God had given? He said that the moment they eat of the fruit, they would be doomed to die. Now Adam and Eve didn't drop dead right then, but God did say that they would eventually die physically. But even more significant than their eventual physical death is the fact that as a result of their disobedience, God no longer allowed them to eat from the *Tree of Life*. This is huge! Remember, the Tree of Life represented the eternal life that God wanted to share with Adam and Eve. Now, through their disobedience, they were no longer allowed to eat from the very tree that enabled them to share in God's own life. Now they were *spiritually dead*. Through their sin, they lost access to God's own life, and they *died* spiritually. And if that wasn't bad enough, this sin affected the state of all mankind; all of the descendants of Adam and Eve would inherit this condition of being spiritually dead, separated from God, and without access to eternal life. This state or condition is what the Church calls *original sin*.

It's important to realize that this state of original sin is a condition of the soul being spiritually dead because of the loss of sanctifying grace. Original sin is not a personal sin that you and I commit; it is a condition in which we find ourselves, the condition of being without the grace that God gives us to share in His divine life. (This is why Adam and Eve's sin is called "the fall." Through their sin, they *fell* from the elevated state to which God had raised them by grace.)

As a result of the sin of our first parents, we have inherited a fallen human nature stained by original sin, and we are in need of being saved and restored to communion with God. Thanks be to God, our heavenly Father didn't (and doesn't) give up on us. He sent His own Son to redeem us and bring us back to the *Tree of Life* so that we can, once again, share in the eternal life that He intended for us in the beginning. In a way, all of salvation history can be simply understood as the story of God's love continually reaching out to us to restore us to the state of grace and holiness that we lost through sin.

SUGGESTED READING:

CCC 374-421
Peter Kreeft, *Fundamentals of the Faith*
Frank Sheed, *Theology for Beginners*
Alan Schreck, *The Essential Catholic Catechism*

THINGS TO CONSIDER:

"Freedom attains perfection in its acts when directed toward God, the sovereign Good" (CCC 1744).

"There is no true freedom except in the service of what is good and just. The choice to disobey and do evil is an abuse of freedom and leads to 'slavery of sin'" (CCC 1733).

"Charity is the theological virtue by which we love God above all things for His own sake, and our neighbor as ourselves for the love of God" (CCC 1822).

"Man, tempted by the devil, let his trust in his Creator die in his heart and, abusing his freedom, disobeyed God's command. This is what man's first sin consisted of. All subsequent sin would be disobedience toward God and lack of trust in His goodness" (CCC 397).

"[Adam] has transmitted to us a sin with which we are all born afflicted, a sin which is the 'death of the soul'" (CCC 403).

"Sanctifying grace is the gratuitous gift of His life that God makes to us; it is infused by the Holy Spirit into the soul to heal it from sin and to sanctify it" (CCC 2023).

In Revelation 2:7, God makes the following promise to those who persevere in the faith, "To the victor I will give the right to eat from the tree of life that is in the garden of God."

WHAT IS THE UNFORGIVABLE SIN?

IN BRIEF:

The unforgivable sin is the rejection of the saving work of God. Jesus says that when we attribute the work of God to the Devil (Beelzebul in Mark 3:22), we are refusing to recognize God's mercy that has come to save us from sin and the Evil One. Such a refusal of grace is unforgivable not because God is unwilling to forgive us, but because we refuse to acknowledge what He is doing in our midst. God's mercy is greater than any sin of ours, but we must be open to receiving God's gift of forgiveness if we are to be truly set free. So, in reality, the only unforgivable sin is the one that we refuse to acknowledge before our merciful Father.

IN DEPTH:

One of the basic truths of the Gospel is that Jesus came to take away the sins of the world and to reconcile us to the Father. We believe that God's mercy is infinitely greater than our sin and that no one is beyond the reach of God's love and forgiveness. But then we come across this interesting place in the Gospel of Mark where Jesus refers to an unforgivable (and everlasting) sin: "Whoever blasphemes against the Holy Spirit will never have forgiveness, but is guilty of an everlasting sin" (Mark 3:29). Jesus seems to be saying pretty clearly that there is some sin that is unforgivable. But what is it, and why is it unforgivable?

Well, to understand what Jesus is talking about we need to step back, look at the rest of the story, and understand what was going on when Jesus said these words. When we look at a Scripture verse without knowing when it was said, to whom it was said, and the circumstances of the event, we can easily misunderstand (and misinterpret) that verse. Looking at Mark 3:20-30 will give us a fuller context within which to understand Jesus' statement. (You may want to read it before going on.)

In Mark 3:20 we see that Jesus was going around casting out demons from people who were possessed and that some of the religious leaders of the Jews began to tell others that it was Jesus who was possessed, and that it was through the power of Satan (Beelzebul) that Jesus was able to cast out these demons.

After first explaining that Satan casting out Satan would make no sense, Jesus utters the verse which refers to this unforgivable sin, the verse we are discussing here specifically. In the footnotes to the New American Bible on Mark 3:29, it says, "This sin is called an everlasting sin because it attributes to Satan, who is the power of evil, what is actually the work of the Holy Spirit."

Basically, the people were claiming that the work of the Holy Spirit was actually the work of Satan. Now, we need to realize that Jesus came for the very purpose of doing God's work (to show us the Father's great love and to forgive us of the sin that keeps us separated from Him). If we fail to recognize and acknowledge that work, we are essentially closing ourselves off from the very mercy and forgiveness that God is trying to bring us. If that is the case, how can we be forgiven? If we think that the work of God is actually the work of the Devil, then we are denying God's power to act and refusing to accept what God is trying to do in our lives. How can we be forgiven if we refuse to acknowledge His ability and desire to forgive us?

Basically, it comes down to this: when we don't believe that God can or will save us, we are closing our hearts to the Holy Spirit, and God can't save us. When we think that the work of God is actually the work of the Evil One, we are placing ourselves outside of the realm of God's mercy and forgiveness. Unless we are open to receiving the mercy and forgiveness that God offers, we can't receive it. It's not that God is unwilling; it is that *we* are unwilling. A great way to state this simply is: *The only sin that God can't or won't forgive is the one that we refuse to ask forgiveness for.*

SUGGESTED READING:
CCC 1864
Mark 3:20-30
Scott Hahn, *Lord Have Mercy: The Healing Power of Confession*

THINGS TO CONSIDER:

"By despair, man ceases to hope for his personal salvation from God, for help in attaining it or for the forgiveness of his sins. Despair is contrary to God's goodness, to His justice – for the Lord is faithful to His promise – and to His mercy" (CCC 2091).

"There are no limits to the mercy of God, but anyone who deliberately refuses to accept His mercy by repenting, rejects the forgiveness of his sins and the salvation offered by the Holy Spirit. Such hardness of heart can lead to final impenitence and eternal loss" (CCC 1864).

WHAT IS THE DIFFERENCE BETWEEN MORTAL SINS AND VENIAL SINS?

IN BRIEF:

All sins have damaging effects on our relationship with God, but some sins (which the Church calls *mortal*) can actually cut us off from the grace of God, and when our soul is cut off from God, it is literally dead. For a sin to be considered a mortal sin, it must be a *serious offense* against God's law that is *freely done* with *full knowledge* of its sinfulness. Sins of this nature cut us off from God not because God rejects us, but because by doing them, we are choosing to reject God and separate ourselves from Him. Sins that are not mortal are called *venial*. Venial sins do not cut us off completely from God but they still damage our ability to fully live in God's grace.

IN DEPTH:

All of our actions have consequences, no matter what we do. Whether they are good or bad, our actions affect both us and the people around us. When we do what is right and good, it actually makes us better people. Like anything, practice makes perfect. When we do what is right, even in the small things, it makes us better equipped to continue to do good in the future; we develop the *habit* of right behavior. This is what it means to grow in virtue, to grow in our ability and readiness to do what is right and good. But, unfortunately, it works the other way as well. When we do things that are not so good, or even down right bad, it harms us and our relationship with others.

Now, it is important to understand that all sins are bad. All sins have a negative effect on us and on our relationship with God but some sins are more harmful than others. Some are so harmful, in fact, that they can actually be deadly. Now this doesn't necessarily mean that if we do certain things we will suddenly drop dead. What it does mean is that there are some sins that actually cause us to die spiritually. These sins that cause us to die spiritually are what the Church calls *mortal* sins. The sins that are harmful but not deadly are what the Church calls *venial* sins. Let's take a look at the difference between them.

When we are baptized, the stain of original sin (the condition of being without God's grace and spiritually dead) is washed away; we become adopted children of God and receive sanctifying grace (which places us in a condition of friendship and holiness before God). Through faith and the sacraments we are given new life, a share in God's own divine life. The goal of our lives is to take active steps to make sure that we grow in holiness and preserve this gift of sanctifying grace. When we sin, this relationship of grace is damaged. Think of the life of grace as a huge pipe connecting us to God, and that through this pipe God's life (grace) flows into our lives. Now, when we sin, we damage this pipe, putting holes in it and clogging it up so that God's grace is hindered in its ability to reach us. We still remain connected to God, but our sin has limited the ability of God's grace to fully reach us and bear fruit in our lives. These sins that damage our relationship with God but still leave us connected to Him are what the Church calls *venial sins*. There are other sins that cause the pipe to be broken entirely. When this happens, our lifeline to God is essentially cut off, and we completely lose access to the grace of God's divine life. These sins that break (or cut off) our relationship with God are what the Church calls *mortal sins*. They are deadly because they result in a loss of the life of grace that God has given to us. But how do we know the difference? How do we know whether a sin is mortal or venial?

The Church teaches that there are three questions that must be considered in order to determine if a sin is a *mortal* sin:

- **Is it of grave matter?** In other words is it a serious offense against a direct commandment of God? A great guideline in determining if a sin is of grave matter is the Ten Commandments (Exodus 20:3-17; Deuteronomy 5:7-21). You have to consider the sin itself (Is it a serious offense against God's law?), but you also have to consider who is harmed by the sin (A sin against one's parents would be more grave than a sin against a stranger.), as well as the damage caused by it (For example, stealing $20,000 from your boss would be more grave than stealing a pencil from work.). Basically, for a sin to be of grave matter it must be a major offense against God's law that does serious harm.

- **Do I have full knowledge of the sinfulness of the act?** Having full knowledge means knowing that what you are doing is a sin, and that it has serious negative effects on your relationship with God. For example, if someone was never taught that *contraception* (artificial birth control) is a sin and contrary to God's plan for sex, that person might not be fully culpable (culpable means *deserving of blame*) for their sin. This wouldn't change the nature of the sin, but it may affect the degree to which the person has their sin held against them in the eyes of God.

- **Was the sin performed with willful consent?** Willful consent means that the action was freely done as a result of a conscious decision. Actions that are forced upon someone (for example, at gunpoint), or actions that are done in a state of impairment (for example, under the influence of drugs/alcohol; or as a result of psychological distress) can limit the degree to which the person is culpable for their sin. Again, this does not mean that the action is not a sin; it means that the person may not be fully responsible for their action because it did not constitute a deliberately free and conscious decision on their part.

For a sin to be considered a mortal sin **ALL THREE** of these conditions must be present. A sin is mortal only if it is of grave matter, **and** you have full knowledge of its sinfulness, **and** if you freely choose to do it. If anyone one of these conditions is not met, the sin would be considered venial. All sins that are not mortal are venial.

What this means is that two people could perform the same sin (let's assume it is of grave matter), but only one of them might be guilty of committing a mortal sin. If one commits the sin with full knowledge and willful consent, but the other person does not have full knowledge that what they are doing is a sin, the first person would be guilty of a mortal sin while the second person would be guilty of a venial sin. This lack of full knowledge doesn't change the fact that *objectively speaking* the acts are equally sinful, but it does diminish the degree to which that person is held morally accountable for their sin.

Jesus told His disciples an interesting parable that speaks to this point. He talked about two servants, one who "knew his master's will" and one who did not. He said that "the servant who knew his master's will but did not make preparations nor act in accord with his will shall be beaten severely, and the servant who was ignorant of his master's will but acted in a way deserving of a severe beating shall be beaten only lightly" (for the whole story, check out Luke 12:35-48). In this story we see Jesus acknowledging that objectively speaking (by looking only at what was done), both servants were deserving of a severe beating, but that when considering how much they knew of the master's will, the one who had full knowledge was held more accountable for his sin. Again, the thing to keep in mind in all of this is that all three conditions must be met for a sin to be mortal.

Now, it might seem harsh to think of God cutting us off completely as a result of a single sinful act. Isn't God all-merciful? Doesn't He forgive all of our sins? The answer to both of these questions is YES! If you think about these three conditions, you can see that they result in destroying our relationship with God not because God cuts us off, but because we choose to cut ourselves off. Mortal sins are deliberate acts against God's law made with the knowledge of their sinfulness and freely done. Essentially, what we are saying to God when we commit a mortal sin is, *I know that what I am doing is a serious offense against Your law and that it will have deadly effects on my relationship with You, but I don't care. I'm going to freely do it anyway.* That's a pretty big rejection of God. When we commit a mortal sin, we are telling God that we don't want the life that He is offering to us; it is us turning away from God, not God turning away from us.

Now what about venial sins? Are they not a big deal? Absolutely not! Remember, all sins are an offense against God and damage our relationship with Him and others. And the more we sin (even venial sins) the weaker our ability to love and serve God becomes. You see, God doesn't want to give us just enough grace to survive; He wants to give us everything that we need to be perfectly holy. But when we sin, we hinder our ability to receive God's grace and allow it to bear fruit in our lives. We must be conscious of all of our sins and seek God's mercy and forgiveness when we fail to love Him and others as we should.

With that said, we must never forget that our God is a God of mercy. He is always ready to give us, once again, the grace of His friendship, even if we have committed a mortal sin. Jesus has given us the Sacrament of Reconciliation to restore the divine life within us (to fix and make perfect the pipe that connects us to God's grace). Venial sins can be forgiven outside of the Sacrament of Reconciliation, for example by receiving the Eucharist, but the Church strongly encourages us to confess our venial sins within the Sacrament of Reconciliation. Mortal sins, on the other hand, must be confessed within the Sacrament of Reconciliation in order for us to receive the sanctifying grace that was lost through mortal sin.

One final thing that is important to keep in mind: while we might be able to look at the actions of others and determine that what they have done is of grave matter (for example, when we hear of someone committing murder), we cannot determine the state of someone's soul. We have no idea to what extent someone has full knowledge of his or her sin or the degree to which they freely chose to commit it. We simply do not know where someone stands in their relationship with God. And so, while we might be able to say objectively that a murderer has committed a grave offense against God's law, we cannot say that person is guilty of a mortal sin, or that they are cut off from God's grace. We entrust all sinners (ourselves included) to the mercy of our loving Father, hoping for their repentance and conversion.

The bottom line is that we should always seek to avoid sin. *All sin* damages our relationship with God and affects our ability to love Him and our neighbor, but there are some sins that involve a direct refusal of God's grace and are called mortal. If we do not repent from them and seek forgiveness, they can kill our soul and keep us eternally separated from God.

SUGGESTED READING:

CCC 1852-1864
Scott Hahn, *Lord Have Mercy*
Dave Armstrong, *The Catholic Verses*
Fr. Mario Romero, *Unabridged Christianity*

THINGS TO CONSIDER:

> *"For a sin to be mortal, three conditions must together be met: 'Mortal sin is sin whose object is grave matter and which is also committed with full knowledge and deliberate consent'"* (CCC 1857).

> *"Unintentional ignorance can diminish or even remove the imputability of a grave offense [...] The promptings of feelings and passions can also diminish the voluntary and free character of the offense, as can external pressures or pathological disorders"* (CCC 1860).

"Venial sin weakens charity; it manifests a disordered affection for created goods; it impedes the soul's progress in the exercise of the virtues and the practice of the moral good [...] Deliberate and unrepented venial sin disposes us little by little to commit mortal sin" (CCC 1863).

"If we acknowledge our sins, He is faithful and just and will forgive our sins and cleanse us from every wrongdoing" (1 John 1:9).

"Although we can judge that an act is in itself a grave offense, we must entrust judgment of persons to the justice and mercy of God" (CCC 1861).

WHY DID JESUS HAVE TO DIE TO SAVE US, AND WHAT ARE WE BEING SAVED FROM?

IN BRIEF:

Sin places a barrier between God and us. As a result of our sin, there is an enormous canyon that separates us from God, and there is absolutely nothing that we can do to reach the other side on our own. However, God's love for us is so great that He chose to build a bridge and close the gap that separates us. Through the life, death, and Resurrection of His own Son, the bridge was made available for us to reach the other side. Jesus does for us what we couldn't do ourselves; being fully human, He was able to offer a perfect sacrifice *on behalf of fallen humanity*. Because He was truly one of us, He could act on our behalf. Because He was also fully divine, the merits or benefits of His sacrifice were of infinite value. Sin had separated us from God, but Jesus' obedience reunited us, and because of His saving work, we now have a way to the other side opened up to us, a way that comes not from our efforts, but from God Himself. What is this way? The way of faith and love, trusting not in our own abilities, but in the grace of God who loves us and restores us to communion with Himself. God asks us to put our faith and trust in Jesus Christ as the Lord of our lives.

IN DEPTH:

No matter who we are or what we believe, we have probably heard, at some point, the phrase "Jesus saves." But when we stop and think about what this means, we are left with a few questions: What does He save us from? Why did He have to do it? And how does He do it? In answering the first question, people will most likely say that Jesus came to save us from hell. This is certainly true, but is that all that it is? Is our salvation just a *get out of hell free* card?

To understand what Jesus saving us means, we need to look at what God intended for us from the beginning. When we look at the first few chapters of Genesis and read the teaching of the *Catechism* on this part of the Bible, we realize that Jesus came to save us from all the effects that our sin and disobedience brought. When God first made Adam and Eve, He made them good and in a right relationship with Him and each other. The

Church calls this state in which Adam and Eve were first made *original justice*. What this original justice means is that when God first made us, our relationship with Him and each other was marked by love and mutual care. This is what God intended for us from the beginning: to live in peace and love with each other and our God.

Then sin happened; through the disobedience of our first parents, all of that was corrupted. We no longer loved God as we were supposed to, and we no longer cared for one another as people made in God's own image. Through sin, this state of original justice was lost, and we found ourselves alienated from God and each other. *This* is why we are in need of salvation. We are not what we were meant to be, and there is nothing that we can do to restore what was lost through sin. Thankfully, as we saw before when we looked at original sin (on page 150), God's love for us is so great that He wished to reach out to us and bring us back to the state of holiness that was lost through sin. So we can see that Jesus came to save us from more than just hell; He came to restore us to a right relationship with God and each other so that we might experience the fullness of life that He intended for us.

God didn't *have* to do this. God had given us all that we needed to live in holiness and peace, but through disobedience (and a lack of trust in God), we turned our back on this great gift. God could have said, "You know what, you had your chance. You're on your own now," but He didn't. Instead He put a plan in motion to save us and restore us to communion with Himself. Sin was a problem that we couldn't fix. There was nothing we could do to reach across the divide that sin had created between God and us. So God, in His wisdom and love, took it upon Himself to solve the problem for us.

How did He do it? Through Jesus Christ – which is why we say "Jesus saves"; it is Jesus who accomplishes what we were unable to do on our own. So from the perspective of God, Jesus didn't have to save us. Nothing obligated God to give us a second chance. It was purely out of love that God freely chose to reach out to us and restore us to His friendship. From our perspective, Jesus had to save us because we were unable to do it ourselves.

So how did Jesus accomplish this? Well, remember that it was through disobedience that grace was lost (through Adam and Eve refusing to follow God's command not to eat from the Tree of Knowledge). Jesus came and gave God the obedience that He asked for. Loving obedience is exactly what God wants from us; He desires to share with us His own life and love, and all He asks of us is to trust in His goodness and obedience to His will.

Jesus is both fully divine and fully human. Jesus is the eternal Word of God made flesh. Because He is the second person of the Trinity He is *fully* divine, but because He assumed human nature and became man He is also *fully* human. This means that Jesus (unlike us) is one divine person with two natures, human and divine. (We have one nature...and by the way, it's human, not divine). So, again motivated solely by love, the eternal Son of God chose to become man so that He could raise up those who had fallen. He did this by offering to His Father a gift of complete obedience on behalf of humanity.

From His willingness to humble Himself and share in our humanity to His obedience even up to the point of death, Jesus offers a pleasing sacrifice to God our Father. Because He was fully human, this sacrifice could be offered on our behalf, and because He was fully divine, this sacrifice was of infinite value. Unlike the disobedience of Adam and Eve, which brought sin and death to humanity, the obedience of Christ brings salvation and new life to all humanity. Jesus essentially stands in our place and does what we were unable to do, which is offer perfect obedience to God. By doing this He provides us with a new way back to the Father, through faith in Jesus Christ, the Word made flesh.

When we say that "Jesus saves," we mean that Jesus brings our soul back to life and restores us to a right relationship with God and each other. Jesus did this through offering Himself as a perfect sacrifice on behalf of fallen mankind, and this sacrifice was so pleasing to God that He has promised those who trust in Christ and follow Him new life through His saving work. Through faith and the sacraments we are made members of the body of Christ (the Church), and so the grace of Christ (the head of the body) overflows to the rest of the body. This is what makes the Good News so good. Through Jesus Christ we have access to new life in the Spirit and can receive once again the grace of sharing in God's own divine life.

SUGGESTED READING:
CCC 899-618
Pope Benedict XVI, *Jesus of Nazareth*
Frank Sheed, *Theology for Beginners*

Peter Kreeft, *Fundamentals of the Faith*
Frank Sheed, *To Know Christ Jesus*

THINGS TO CONSIDER:

"The Church, interpreting the symbolism of Biblical language in an authentic way, in the light of the New Testament and Tradition, teaches that our first parents, Adam and Eve, were constituted in an original 'state of holiness and justice' [...] By the radiance of this grace all dimensions of man's life were confirmed [...] The inner harmony of the human person, the harmony between the first couple and all creation, comprised the state called 'original justice'" (CCC 376).

"After the fall, man was not abandoned by God. On the contrary, God calls him and in a mysterious way heralds the coming victory over evil and his restoration from his fall" (CCC 410).

St. Gregory of Nyssa beautifully says of the coming of Christ, "Sick, our nature demanded to be healed; fallen, to be raised up; dead, to rise again. We had lost the possession of the good; it was necessary for it to be given back to us. Closed in the darkness, it was necessary to bring us the light; captives, we awaited a Savior; prisoners, help; slaves, a liberator. Are these things minor or insignificant? Did they not move God to descend to human nature and visit it, since humanity was in so miserable and unhappy a state?" (CCC 457).

"By His obedience unto death, Jesus accomplishes the substitution of the suffering Servant, who 'makes Himself an offering for sin,' when 'He bore the sin of many,' and who 'shall make many to be accounted righteous,' for 'He shall bear their iniquities.' Jesus atoned for our faults and made satisfaction for our sins to the Father" (CCC 615).

"United with Christ, the Church is sanctified by Him; through Him and with Him she becomes sanctifying" (CCC 824).

WHAT DO "SALVATION" AND "JUSTIFICATION" MEAN?

IN BRIEF:

Salvation is the restoration of what has been lost and damaged by sin. It involves reconciling us to God and healing our broken relationships with Him and one another. Justification is a real internal renewal of sinners that fills them with God's grace and makes them adopted children of God. All of this is made possible through the saving work of Jesus Christ, who frees us from sin and gives us access to new life in the Spirit.

IN DEPTH:

When it comes to our faith, salvation refers to our being saved from the effects of sin. Sin has consequences, the worst of which is separation from God. In addition to damaging our relationship with God, sin also affects our relationships with others and even our relationship with ourselves. Sin affects our relationship with God because it involves a rejection of what He made us to do (which is to know and love Him through seeking what is good and true). Sin affects our relationships with others because it brings manipulation, selfishness, and distrust into them (just think of how becoming known as a "liar" affects our relationships). Sin also affects our relationship with ourselves because it confuses us internally. Because of sin we find ourselves pulled in different directions; our mind might want to do one thing, our body another, and our emotions something else. All of this is brought about by sin.

Salvation, then, is ultimately the restoration of all that has been lost and damaged by sin. Salvation is setting right what was messed up by sin. Most importantly this means that salvation is a restoration of our relationship with God, giving us once again a share in the grace of God's own life. But salvation is also a healing of the wounds caused by sin, which means that it involves restoring us to right relationships with others and a right ordering of our lives.

Another term that is used to capture this idea of being restored to grace and friendship with God is *justification*. St. Paul often speaks about our being "justified" by the saving work of Christ (see Romans 3:24-26). Justification is the action of God that restores us to a life of grace; it makes us pleasing to God and establishes us in a right relationship with Him. In a sense, justification refers to the change that takes place in us when we receive the gift of salvation offered to us though Christ. Ultimately, by God's grace, justification changes us from sinners displeasing to God to adopted children in His family. But is this change something that takes place in us, or is it just a change in the way God sees us?

This may not seem like that important of a question, but our answer to it actually reveals a lot about what we believe salvation to be. Now there are some who would say that what happens in justification is that God just looks at us *as though* we were righteous (or holy). The idea is that Christ alone is righteous, and that through faith in Him, we are considered to be righteous though nothing *actually* changes about us specifically. All that changes is the way that God sees us. Think about it this way: through sin, my soul has become dark and ugly, full of selfishness, greed, and pride. Through faith I am given a beautiful, spotless sheet that covers up my ugliness. This sheet is Christ's own righteousness, which He graciously shares with me. This way, when God looks at me, what He sees is not my sinfulness, but the righteousness of Christ. But, if you were to look under the sheet at any time, you would still see the same dirty, unworthy sinner. This understanding of justification is referred to as *imputed righteousness*; in this view the righteousness of Christ is just counted as being our own. This, however, is not how the Catholic Church understands justification.

It is true that sin has wounded our human nature, and that left to our own ability, none of us could stand before God and be considered holy or righteous. But, as Catholics, we believe that by justification we are not simply covered with Christ's righteousness, but we are actually filled with Christ's righteousness. This view is known as *infused righteousness* because the righteousness of Christ is actually infused into our very soul, bringing about a real change in us. This means that when a just person (someone who has been justified by grace) stands before God, God looks into that person's soul and is pleased with what He sees because that person's soul is actually *filled* (not just covered) with Christ's own righteousness. According to the view of infused righteousness, the just person is considered righteous because they have accepted the gift of God's grace, which has resulted in a real internal renewal and sanctification.

If salvation is a restoration of what sin has lost and damaged, then it makes sense that our justification would be a real healing and transformation of the corruption caused to our souls by sin. God doesn't want to just hide our sinfulness; He wants to take it away. He doesn't want to just look at the medical records of a healthy person and so consider us to be well; He wants to heal us of our sickness.

This is the great gift of salvation and justification; through grace God brings about a real change in us so that we can fully experience the life of holiness that He intended for us from the beginning.

SUGGESTED READING:

CCC 1987-2016
Frank Sheed, *Theology for Beginners*
Scott Hahn, *Lord Have Mercy*
Dave Armstrong, *The Catholic Verses*

THINGS TO CONSIDER:

> *"The harmony in which they had found themselves, thanks to original justice, is now destroyed: the control of the soul's spiritual faculties over the body is shattered; the union of man and woman becomes subject to tensions, their relations henceforth marked by lust and domination. Harmony with creation is broken: visible creation has become alien and hostile to man [...] Finally, the consequence explicitly foretold for this obedience will come true: man will 'return to the ground,' for out of it he was taken. Death makes its entrance into human history" (CCC 400).*

> *Salvation is "the forgiveness of sins and restoration of friendship with God, which can be done by God alone" (CCC Glossary).*

"Justification consists in both victory over death caused by sin and a new participation in grace. It brings about filial adoption so that men become Christ's brethren [...] We are not brethren by nature, but by the gift of grace, because that adoptive filiation gains us a real share in the life of the only Son, which was revealed in His Resurrection" (CCC 654).

Justification is "The gracious action of God which frees us from sin and communicates 'the righteousness of God through faith in Jesus Christ.' Justification in not only the remission of sins, but also the sanctification and renewal of the interior man" (CCC Glossary).

HOW ARE WE SAVED? (FAITH VS. WORKS)

IN BRIEF:

Some people would like to say that we are saved by faith alone. But did you know that the phrase "faith alone" is only used once in the Bible, and that when it is used, it actually says that we are not saved by faith alone (James 2:24)? So then how are we saved? It is through what St. Paul calls the obedience of faith. God has made salvation possible by the life, death, and Resurrection of Jesus. But this gift of salvation must be received in order for us to actually be saved. How do we receive it? By repentance (acknowledging our sin), faith (trusting in Jesus as the source of new life in the Spirit), and works of love and obedience (seeking to live according to the way of the Gospel). Both faith without works and works without faith are lifeless and cannot save us. It is only faith working through love, faith that is lived out through love and obedience to the one in whom we place our faith, that we can be saved. It is *both* faith *and* works that saves us.

IN DEPTH:

The answer to this question brings us to one of the biggest areas of disagreement between Catholic and non-Catholic Christians. In the 16th century, a man named Martin Luther ended up breaking away from the Catholic Church because of disagreements over certain teachings, and this very issue (concerning the nature of justification or how we are saved) was one of the central areas of contention. From his study of the Bible, Martin Luther believed that the essential teaching of the New Testament was that we are justified (or saved) by faith alone, and that over time, the Catholic Church had corrupted this teaching by focusing too much on good works in the process of justification. So, this question about how we are saved goes to the very heart of the issues that divide Catholic and non-Catholic Christians.

The question here is, ultimately, about the relationship between faith and works. Non-Catholics will often say that Catholics believe that they can earn their salvation by doing good works, and this, they say, goes directly against what St. Paul says in his letter to the Ephesians, "By grace you have been saved through faith, and this is not from you; it is the gift of God; it is not from works, so no one may boast" (Ephesians 2:8-9). This seems pretty clear right? St. Paul says that we are saved by grace, through faith, and that all of this is a gift from God, not something that we have earned. So, do Catholics believe this teaching of St. Paul? Of course! We believe that the work of salvation that God accomplished through Jesus Christ is a free gift that we did not earn.

There is nothing that we did, or could have done, to obligate God to come down and save us. It's not as though God was sitting up in heaven and said, "You know, they've just been so good that I have to do this." No, God freely chose to take the steps necessary to reconcile us to Himself, not because we were so good, but because He is so good. It was solely God's love and goodness that moved Him to reach out to us and save us. This is why St. Paul says that it is by grace that we have been saved, because this gift is undeserved and freely given to us by God.

So now, if all of this is a free gift, where do works fit in? Well, the important question we have to ask is how do we receive this gift? A gift has to be accepted for it to be enjoyed as it was intended. If someone refuses to accept a gift, they lose out on the opportunity to enjoy what that gift was meant to bring. Well, Jesus' offer of salvation is no different. Through His life, death, and Resurrection He offers to all of us the gift of new life as children of God. In order for this gift to take effect in our lives, we have to accept the gift that He offers.

Now, many people would say that this gift of salvation is accepted by accepting Christ as their personal Lord and Savior. The idea here is that after acknowledging their sinfulness and their need for a savior, they come to accept Christ as their only savior and put all their trust in His saving work as the source of their salvation. That's it. Nothing more is needed. It is not through anything that they do, but only through their faith in what Jesus has done, that they are saved. According to this view, someone's good works don't have anything to do with their salvation; it is only that person's faith in Jesus Christ that saves them. This all sounds like the logical conclusion of Ephesians 2:8-9.

So then what's wrong with this view? Well, let me first explain what is right with it. As we said before, the gift of salvation that God offers to us is a free gift and nothing that we have earned. And this gift does require a response that involves accepting Christ as the savior of our lives by faith and living with Him as the Lord of our lives. But, we run into a problem when we begin to say that our works don't matter, that there is nothing that we have to do other than have faith in Christ. The first problem is that strictly speaking, putting our faith in Christ is something that we do, so can we really say that none of our works matter? There is at least something that we have to do in order to be saved. But a second (and bigger) problem is that there are other places in the New Testament where the importance of our good works are emphasized. For example, St. Paul tells the Romans that God, "will repay everyone according to His works: eternal life to those who seek glory, honor, and immortality through perseverance in good works, but wrath and fury to those who selfishly disobey the truth and obey wickedness" (Romans 2:6-8). Also, in James we read that "faith of itself, if it does not have works, is dead." In fact, later on it specifically says that we are saved by works and not by faith alone. But wait, didn't St. Paul say that we are saved by faith and not by works? How can St. James be saying that we are saved by works and not by faith alone? Is the Bible contradicting itself here? No! But then how can we make sense of both of these passages?

Well, we have to go back to how the Catholic Church understands our acceptance of God's gift of salvation. Remember, the gift of salvation is just that, a gift; our works have nothing to do with the gift being offered in the first place, but the gift does require a response. The beginning of this response is repentance (acknowledging our sin and our need for a savior) and faith (trusting that Jesus Christ has died for our sins and is the way back to the Father). But this isn't the end of the story. You see, faith is more than just believing something to be true (for example, believing that Jesus died for my sins and that by His death I have been given new life). Faith is a way of life. In fact, in St. Paul's letter to the Romans the very first and last time that the word "faith" is used it is joined to another word: "obedience" (Romans 1:5, 16:26). St. Paul says that he has been sent to bring about the "obedience of faith" among all the nations. Obedience and faith go hand in hand, so much so that you could say that the one makes manifest the other. This is why Jesus says, "if you love me you will keep my commandments" (John 14:15). When we recognize the great gift that Jesus has given to us, it should move us to respond not just with faith, but with lives of loving obedience to what God asks of us. Our faith should be "working through love" as St. Paul says to the Galatians (Galatians 5:6). Our faith in Christ as our Lord and Savior should move us to live according to the way of life that this faith entails. If our faith doesn't do this, what good is it? Can faith that isn't lived out in good works save us? St. James says no (check out James 2:14-26). But then how do we make sense of St. Paul's teaching that we are saved by faith and not by works?

While at first these two ideas seem to contradict each other, they are in fact making the same point in different ways. St. Paul is saying that works, if they are not done as a result of faith, cannot save us. Why? Because we can never earn our salvation by our works alone. If we approach God thinking that we have done enough good works to earn our way into heaven, we are going to be seriously disappointed. There is no amount of good works that could ever put God in the position of being obligated to give us salvation. Again, salvation is a gift. And this gift is accepted by faith and trust in the One who gives the gift. So, according to St. Paul, works without faith cannot save us. St. James, on the other hand, is saying that faith that is not lived out through works of love and obedience is a dead faith. Why? Because loving obedience to God is the proper response to the gift that He has given to us. To say that we trust in Jesus but then refuse to live according to the Gospel that He preached doesn't do us any good. Because of this, according to St. James, faith without works cannot save us.

So then what does save us? Faith and works together: the obedience of faith or faith working through love. While it is true that our works (separated from faith) cannot save us, our works that are done out of faith do save us. In fact, our faith is what gives our works the ability to have value in the eyes of God. When our works are done as an expression of our faith (seeking to always be conscious of our sin and our need for God's grace for all that we are and do), and in cooperation with the Holy Spirit (who Jesus sent to guide our lives according to the way of the Gospel), God our loving Father can accept our efforts (though imperfect) and be pleased with them. He accepts them not because they are, strictly speaking, good enough but because they are done out of love for Him and in response to the gift of new life that He has given us. Through faith (and Baptism) we become members of God's family, and through our works, we show that we are willing to live as true children of God. Without faith we could never enter into God's family, but without works we could never show our gratitude for being allowed to be a part of God's family in the first place. While faith is absolutely necessary for salvation, this faith must be lived out in loving and faithful obedience to the One who saves us. We are not saved by faith alone, but faith working through love (faith and works).

SUGGESTED READING:

CCC 2006-2016
James 2:14-26
Romans 1-8
Fr. Mario Romero, *Unabridged Christianity*
The Staff of Catholic Answers, *The Essential Catholic Survival Guide*
Dave Armstrong, *The Catholic Verses*

THINGS TO CONSIDER:

> "Since the initiative belongs to God in the order of grace, no one can merit the initial grace of forgiveness and justification, at the beginning of conversion" (CCC 2010).

> "Our justification comes from the grace of God. Grace is favor, the free and undeserved help that God gives us to respond to His call to be children of God, adoptive sons, partakers in the divine nature and of eternal life" (CCC 1996).

> "See how a person is justified by works and not by faith alone" (James 2:24).

> "I [...] urge you to live in a manner worthy of the call you have received" (Ephesians 4:1).

> "The charity of Christ is the source in us of all our merits before God. Grace, by uniting us to Christ in active love, ensures the supernatural quality of our acts and consequently their merit before God and before men" (CCC 2011).

> "You are glorified in the assembly of your Holy Ones, for in crowning their merits you are crowing your own gifts" (CCC 2013).

ARE CATHOLICS "SAVED"?

IN BRIEF:

Many Christians believe that accepting Christ as your personal Lord and Savior is how you are saved. Now, while accepting Christ as the Lord of your life is certainly essential and indispensable to the Christian life (yes, for Catholics too), this is not an event that happens some time in the past; it is an ongoing commitment to live with Jesus Christ as the center of your life. It is through this ongoing commitment to the *obedience of faith* (Romans 1:5, 15:26) that the gift of salvation offered to us through Jesus is able to reach its completion in heaven (which is when we will be "saved" in the complete and definitive sense). So, technically speaking, we would say that Catholics are saved because by the life, death, and Resurrection of Christ, they have been set free from sin and death. Through the work of grace and the gifts of the Holy Spirit, they are *being saved*, as they conform daily to the holiness that God intends for them; and they *will be saved* because through perseverance in faith and love, they will one day arrive at the fullness of salvation in the joy of heaven.

IN DEPTH:

Have you ever been asked, "Are you saved?" If you have and you are Catholic, there is a pretty good chance that you may have stumbled to give an answer. Other similar questions that you may have been asked are, "Have you accepted Jesus Christ as your personal Lord and Savior?" or "Are you born again?" Again, these are questions that many Catholics might not exactly know how to answer. But why? Why do these questions strike us Catholics as somewhat odd? Well, it's not because we don't believe in salvation (we do) or because we have a problem with saying that Jesus is our Lord and Savior (He is). Ultimately, it is because we understand "being saved" in a specific way. Strictly speaking, being saved is not something that we experience in this life (although it certainly begins here); it is something that happens after this life is over.

Jesus came to save us, which we know. But what is this "salvation" that He came to bring? Well, to put it simply, it is to enable us to do what God intended for us from the beginning: to live eternally in communion with God, to share in the life and love of the Trinity (for more on this, check out the question "What is the purpose of life?" on page 38). This is why God made us, but sin stood in the way of this actually taking place. Therefore, Jesus came to take away the sin of the world so that we could, once again, have access to God's own divine life and be enabled to live eternally with Him. The final goal or purpose of salvation is for us to live forever with God in the joy of heaven. But this means that our salvation is not complete until we are in heaven; only then are we truly saved definitively and unquestionably.

Now, it is true that when we believe in Christ and are baptized, we truly are reborn as children of God and experience *in this life* a share in God's own life. But this is only the beginning and a foretaste of the fullness of salvation that awaits us in heaven. Through faith and the sacraments, we truly do come to share in the new life of the risen Christ, but it is not until the joy of heaven that we will experience this life in its fullness. So, in a certain sense, the only people who are saved are those who have already died and are living in the joy of heaven (such as the saints).

When most people say that they are "saved," they are not understanding it in this way. What they usually mean is that they have accepted Christ as their Lord and Savior, and so they consider themselves among those who have been saved by Christ's death and Resurrection. The idea is that by accepting Christ, one is saved or born again, and that those who are saved have a sort of "reserved seat" in heaven. In fact, some (but not all) Christians believe that once you are saved (once you have accepted Christ), you are *guaranteed* a place in heaven, and that there is nothing that you could ever do that would prevent you from getting there. (This idea is often embodied in the phrase "once saved, always saved.")

Okay, so what about being "saved" in this sense? Are Catholics saved? If by this you mean have they accepted Christ as their Lord and Savior? I certainly hope so! But this is not something that happens at one moment in time in the past; it is something that has to be done daily (or even hourly). You see, at every moment, in every decision that we make, we have a choice: do we live with Christ as the Lord of our lives, or do we let something or someone else take His place? "Accepting Christ" isn't a one-time deal. It is a lifelong commitment, one that requires us to renew this commitment daily. Just because we accepted Christ as Lord last month doesn't necessarily mean that we are going to allow Him to be Lord of our lives today. At any moment, we could say, *you know what, forget it, I don't want You to be Lord of my life, I am taking back the controls.*

Now, this brings us right to the issue mentioned above: is it possible for someone who is saved (or born again) to lose their salvation? While some Christians say that it is not, as Catholics we believe that although we receive the gift of new life in the Spirit and the grace needed to persevere in the faith, we are free to turn our backs on the gift that we have been given at any time. Think of it in terms of a family. As children of God, we enjoy the love, grace, and mercy of our loving Father, as well as the promised inheritance of eternal life. As long as we remain in the family (through steadfast faith and obedience to the way of life that God asks of us, and repentance when we fall short of this standard), then the inheritance is ours. But at any moment we can choose to run away from home, to reject our place in the family of God (for example, through mortal sin). If this happens, then we can forfeit our inheritance and lose the eternal life that God wishes to give us. So, even though faith and Baptism makes us children of God and heirs of eternal life, there is nothing that forces us to retain our place in God's family. At any moment, we are free to disinherit ourselves. Again, this is because we are not ultimately and definitively saved until we are living eternally with God in the joy of heaven.

So then, how should we, as Catholics, answer this question of whether or not we are saved? Well, our answer is three-fold: we have been saved, we are being saved, and we will be saved as long as we stay in God's good grace. We *are saved* because Christ has set us free from sin and death through His life, death, and Resurrection; We are *being saved* because we are being continually renewed and restored to the holiness that God intended for us from the beginning; and we *will be saved* if we remain faithful to God who is guiding us to our homeland in heaven.

SUGGESTED READING:
CCC 162-165, 1002-1004
Fr. Mario Romero, *Unabridged Christianity*
The Staff of Catholic Answers, *The Essential Catholic Survival Guide*
Dave Armstrong, *The Catholic Verses*

THINGS TO CONSIDER:

"Faith makes us taste in advance the light of the beatific vision, the goal of our journey here below. Then we shall see God 'face to face,' 'as He is.' So faith is already the beginning of eternal life" (CCC 163).

"Faith is an entirely free gift that God makes to man. We can lose this precious gift [...] To live, grow, and persevere in the faith until the end we must nourish it with the word of God; we must beg the Lord to increase our faith, it must be 'working through charity,' abounding in hope, and rooted in the faith of the Church" (CCC 162).

DO YOU HAVE TO BE CHRISTIAN TO GO TO HEAVEN?

IN BRIEF:

Jesus made it very clear that He is the one and only way to the Father. It is only through the saving life, death, and Resurrection of Jesus Christ and a living faith in Him that we have the ability to reach our home in heaven. However, the Church also teaches that God is able to lead to Himself those who, though not officially professing to be Christian, are nonetheless seeking God through doing their best to live according to truth and goodness. This isn't because being Christian doesn't really matter, but because God's grace is without limit. This possibility also doesn't diminish our responsibility to make Christ known, since through Him we have been given the clear path that leads to heaven. Even though someone outside of this path may be able to make it, we are obligated to show others the true path of salvation because it is only on this path that we can be sure that we are moving toward God and eternal life.

IN DEPTH:

Before answering this question specifically, we first need to be clear on one important point. *If* non-Christians do get to heaven, it will have been possible only because of the saving life, death, and Resurrection of Jesus Christ. It is very important that we understand this: Jesus is the source of our salvation, and He is the only way to the Father and the one Savior of the world. This means that everyone who is saved is saved *by Christ*. Jesus isn't the way to heaven just for Christians; He is *the* way to heaven, period.

So, our answer to this question must keep this truth in mind. If non-Christians make it to heaven, it won't be because they have found some other way or a secret, unguarded back entrance. Heaven is made possible *only* through the saving work of Jesus Christ and the gift of grace that comes *through Him* into the world.

With this in mind, let's take a look at the original question, "Do you have to be Christian to get to heaven?" The simple answer is no. It is *possible* that people who do not formally profess to be Christians in this life can still make it to heaven. Why? Because God is God. Nothing is impossible for God, and we shouldn't pretend to think that we know what God can and cannot do. The Bible says that "the hand of the Lord is not too short to save" (Isaiah 59:1). Only God knows a person's soul. We have no idea to what extent someone has accepted or rejected God's invitation to grace. What we do know is that we have a loving and merciful God, and we trust that He extends to everyone at least the possibility to be saved.

Now, with that being said, saying that it is possible for a non-Christian to get to heaven is *not* the same as saying that it doesn't matter whether or not someone is a Christian. Just because God *could* save someone who is not a Christian doesn't mean that being Christian doesn't matter. You see, God wants us to get to heaven. This is why He continued to reach out to Adam and Eve and their descendants after the fall, why He chose to reveal His law to the people of Israel in the Old Testament, why He sent His own Son as the fullness of revelation in the New Testament, and why He sent forth the apostles with a message of salvation meant for all people. All of this was done because God *wants* us to live with Him forever in the joy of heaven. Because of this, God chose to show us the clear path that leads to Him.

So what does this path look like? It involves faith and trust in Jesus Christ as the source of new life. It involves entering into communion with His body (the Church) through Baptism, continuing to grow in holiness through participating in the sacraments, and living out our faith according to the way of the Gospel, through love of God and love of neighbor. In other words, this path to heaven is the path of Christianity. Essentially, Jesus came to show us that He is the way to heaven, and if we follow Him and stay on the path that He sets before us, He will lead us to our true home. Remember, God wants us to make it, so He sent Jesus to show us the clear path that would lead us there. As long as we do our best to follow Christ and stay on this path, we trust that we will make it by the help of the Holy Spirit.

This is why being Christian is so important. Because it is the way that Jesus promised would lead us to heaven. Now, someone who is not on this path but is still trying to head in the direction of God may, in fact, be able to reach their destination by God's grace. But then again, they may not. When we are not on the path that Jesus made for us, things aren't as clear. We can become confused about the direction that we are supposed to be traveling and may even spend a great deal of time going the wrong way. When we are off the main road, we can't always be sure where we are going to end up. God may be able to still guide us in the right direction, but the path itself may be far less clear. Again, God's grace has no limits. We hope and trust that He is at work trying to draw all people to Himself so that they might come to know the truth and live in His love. Because of this hope, we acknowledge that it is possible for non-Christians to be saved, but we also recognize that He has given us a path to Himself that we can trust. Through faith in Christ and obedience to the Gospel, we are set on the clear (though not easy) path that leads to heaven.

Now, with this being said, we need to be careful to avoid a serious error here: it would be wrong to say that Christianity is just one way to God among many other equally valuable options. No, Jesus (and Christianity) is *the way* to heaven. It is through faith in Jesus Christ and following the way of the Gospel that we are given the sure path that leads to salvation. Therefore, even though God may be able to guide to Himself those who are seeking to live according to truth and goodness, this does not diminish the importance of bearing witness to the Jesus Christ as the one Savior of the world and the only one who can bring us to heaven.

SUGGESTED READING:
Ad Gentes
Lumen Gentium, Chapter II

THINGS TO CONSIDER:

> *"I am the way and the truth and the life. No one comes to the Father except through Me" (John 14:6).*

> *"There is no salvation through anyone else, nor is there any other name under heaven given to the human race by which we are to be saved" (Acts 4:12).*

> *"It must be firmly believed as a truth of Catholic faith that the universal salvific will of the One and Triune God is offered and accomplished once for all in the mystery of the Incarnation, death, and Resurrection of the Son of God" (Dominus Iesus, 14).*

"Since Christ died for all, and since all men are in fact called to one and the same destiny, which is divine, we must hold that the Holy Spirit offers to all the possibility of being made partners, in a way known to God, in the paschal mystery" (Gaudium et Spes, 22).

"Those who, through no fault of their own, do not know the Gospel of Christ or His Church, but who nevertheless seek God with a sincere heart, and, moved by grace, try in their actions to do His will as they know it through the dictates of their conscious – those too may achieve eternal salvation" (Lumen Gentium, 16).

"Everyone, therefore, ought to be converted to Christ, who is known through the preaching of the Church, and they ought, by Baptism, to become incorporated into Him, and into the Church which is His body" (Ad Gentes, 7).

"Although in ways known to Himself God can lead those who, through no fault of their own, are ignorant of the Gospel to that faith without which it is impossible to please Him, the Church, nevertheless, still has the obligation and also the sacred right to evangelize" (Ad Gentes, 7).

WHAT IS HEAVEN LIKE?

IN BRIEF:

Heaven will be unlike anything that we can imagine. The Bible says that our hearts and minds can't even begin to conceive of what the joy of heaven will look like. The Bible also tells us that it will be the satisfaction of our deepest longings. In heaven we will experience the very life and love of the Trinity and be united with all of our brothers and sisters in Christ. While we don't know exactly what this will be like, since we were made by God and for God, we know that heaven will be an eternal state of happiness and communion with the Father, Son, and Holy Spirit, and it will be the fulfillment of our very being.

IN DEPTH:

Honestly, no one can really tell you what it's going to look like or what we are going to do in heaven. While we could try to give you some description that sounds good in the hope of making you really want to go there, we simply don't know the details of what it will be like. Now, we know that's not very inspiring, but don't get too discouraged yet. Just because we can't *describe* it doesn't mean that we can't say anything about it at all.

So what do we know about heaven?

Firstly, we have to remember why God made us in the first place. God is perfect, life-giving love. From all eternity, God is a communion of love between the Father, Son, and Holy Spirit. God is lacking in nothing; He is truth, goodness, beauty, peace, etc. However, for some reason (that reason being love), God freely chose to create us so that we might be invited to share in what He is by nature. God made us to share in the very life and love of the Trinity. Heaven is, ultimately, the attainment of that goal. In heaven we will participate in God's own life, which means that we will come to share in the truth, goodness, beauty, peace, and love of the Trinity. We will live with Him forever and enjoy all that He is. Since this was the very reason for our existence, we know that heaven will be the fulfillment of our deepest longing and desires.

The Bible also tells us that in heaven we will see God "face to face" (1 Corinthians 13:12). The idea here is that we will see God in an intensely intimate way with nothing blurring our vision or preventing us from experiencing Him as He truly is. The fancy theological name for this is the *beatific vision*. In the beatific vision, we will see and experience God in a way that is far greater than anything we experience here on earth. Heaven will surpass anything that we have known in this life, for we will see God in all of His glory and share in His divinity.

The Church also teaches that in heaven we will experience a deep sense of communion with all of our brothers and sisters in faith. Through faith we know that death is not the end of the story; those who have died with Christ will also live with Him in glory. In heaven, we will be joined to all those who have walked the path of faith throughout history. Can you imagine seeing our relatives, our guardian angel, and the great saints of the Old and New Testament? In heaven we will be united to them as a result of our union with God. That communion will be greater than any friendship or love that we have experienced or will ever experience in this life.

In the attempt to describe heaven, the most common image used is that of a *wedding feast*. Now, this is surely a figurative description, but it helps give us an image of heaven as being full of joy, celebration, gladness, fulfillment, union, love, and abundance, all of which are ways of showing us that heaven will be a time of great joy and deep fulfillment.

In St. Paul's letter to the Corinthians he says, "no eye has seen, nor ear heard, nor the heart of man conceived, what God has prepared for those who love Him" (1 Corinthians 2:9). We can't even imagine what heaven will actually be like. It is truly beyond our wildest dreams, unlike anything we have ever seen and beyond anything that we can think of. It will be everything we have ever wanted; it will be the fulfillment of everything we have ever longed for; it will be the satisfaction of our deepest longing; it will be a joyful resting in the love and goodness of the God who made us to know Him and share in His life. While I can't imagine what this will be like, I know that it's where I want to be, and I will trust in God for the rest.

SUGGESTED READING:

CCC 1023-1029
Scott Hahn, *The Lamb's Supper*
Frank Sheed, *Theology for Beginners*
Peter Kreeft, *Catholic Christianity*, Chapter X

THINGS TO CONSIDER:

"Heaven is the ultimate end and fulfillment of the deepest human longings, the state of supreme, definitive happiness" (CCC 1024).

"Because of His transcendence, God cannot be seen as He is, unless He Himself opens up His mystery to man's immediate contemplation and gives him the capacity for it. The Church calls this contemplation of God in His heavenly glory 'the beatific vision'" (CCC 1028).

"Heaven is the blessed community of all who are perfectly incorporated into Christ" (CCC 1026).

Heaven is *"eternal life with God; communion of life and love with the Trinity and all the blessed. Heaven is the state of supreme and definitive happiness, the goal of the deepest longing of humanity"* (CCC Glossary).

WHY WOULD A LOVING GOD SEND SOMEONE TO HELL?

IN BRIEF:

Many people ask "how can an all-loving God send someone to hell?" That question, actually, has merit. How can God, who is Love (1 John 4:8), *send* a soul to hell for eternity? Properly understood, God does not send people to hell; if a soul ends up in hell it is due to their own choices and sin. God the Father, when He gave us free will, gives us the invitation to heaven, but it's up to us to respond in love. So, in essence, God has never *sent* anyone to hell, but He has allowed souls to turn from Him and end up there.

IN DEPTH:

People use all kinds of excuses not to follow God. One of the most popular is the proposal that the existence of hell must prove that God isn't really loving, for how could a loving Father or Creator allow His children to burn forever in torment? The question demonstrates a false dichotomy. The paradox is actually that hell exists *because* God is *so loving*!

People for centuries have argued that "a loving God" would not allow people to go to hell. Some even argue that hell doesn't exist – that all roads eventually lead to heaven. That idea, however, renders Jesus both a liar and a fraud (Matthew 7:13-14, Matthew 25:31-46).

Hell exists because God is so loving!

Jesus spoke about heaven, hell, and judgment often; He spoke about them lovingly but forcefully – there was no mistaking God. The truth is that hell exists precisely because God is so loving. This is where the confusion sets in.

Let's be clear here: God does not send people to hell. Hell is a decision on our part. Hell is basically a choice that we make, one that God – out of respect for our free will – honors out of His immense love for us.

Put very simply, you can look at it this way:

"Tim" lives his life "his way." He does what he wants – whatever seems to make him happy. He rejects Christ's teachings on faith and morals. He shuts out the people who try to share Christ's love with him. He chooses to do things his way. Tim wants nothing to do with God during his time on earth. When Tim dies, he is judged – according to what he heard and what he was exposed to in terms of God's truth. Tim, living in 21st century America, has lost the excuse of ignorance. He can't pretend he never heard about God, witnessed modern Christians' lives or was never exposed to the truth. Tim's life, however, became his response to the truth of God.

Hell is the absence of God and His love. Hell is a choice on our part. Those souls in hell are eternally removed from God.

God now – out of His immense and unconditional love for Tim – basically says, "Tim, my beloved son, I tried and tried again to reach out to you in love. I shared truth with you. I provided countless opportunities for you to know and love Me… but you rejected Me. So, Tim, since you wanted nothing to do with Me on earth, and that was your choice, I will not force you to spend eternity with Me in heaven. I will honor your free will and allow you to spend eternity where I am not."

And we call that "place" hell.

Hell is the absence of God and His love. Hell is a choice on our part. Those souls in hell are eternally removed from God. There is no way for them to know His love or anything about His plan. They are eternally frustrated. There is no love, no goodness, no beauty, no sacrifice, no peace, and no joy. There is only selfishness, ignorance, bitterness, and hatred. The absence of God is so horrific; we cannot even fathom it. We call it hell, but a simple word or mental picture cannot begin to do justice to this reality.

As much as heaven is the fulfillment of all goodness, knowledge, and love, hell is the opposite. When we die, our wills are set. We have freely chosen in this life whether we want to be with God for all eternity. This isn't like the movies where you "argue your case" before God. Heaven is an invitation into God's life for all eternity. Our lives on earth are like the RSVP. Heaven is an invitation. Hell is a decision.

SUGGESTED READING:

Matthew 22:12-14, 25:41-46
Luke 3:9, 16-17
John 15:6
Isaiah 33:11
Job 1:6-9
2 Kings 1:2-6, 1:16
CCC 1033-36, 1861
Cardinal Joseph Ratzinger (Pope Benedict XVI), *Eschatology*
Peter Kreeft, *Fundamentals of the Faith*

DO CATHOLICS STILL BELIEVE IN PURGATORY AND WHAT IS IT, EXACTLY?

IN BRIEF:

Yes, Catholics still very much believe in Purgatory (Catholics who follow the Church, that is and not "their own" set of beliefs). Purgatory is a temporary state of purification where imperfect saints have the effects of their sin purged.

Consider this analogy. Have you ever tried to put a wrinkled dollar bill into a soda machine? You try your best to straighten it out but the machine simply can't receive it in its wrinkled, tattered state...but if you put in a crisp, new bill it goes right in. Purgatory is where all the "wrinkles" are purged and "ironed out." Remember, the wrinkled dollar is not worth less than the new one it just needs some help. Put simply, Purgatory means you'll get to heaven, some day, but that you have a few things God has to "iron out" first.

IN DEPTH:

Every year around the Feast of All Souls (November 2nd), people begin to ask far more questions regarding the Catholic Church's teaching on Purgatory. Some questions are from cradle Catholics wanting to better understand what we believe. Some questions are from Protestant Christians wanting to know why the Catholic Church "made Purgatory up." Still others are from people wondering if the Church still teaches the doctrine of Purgatory since they don't hear much about it anymore.

The quick answer is "yes," Purgatory is very much a reality. The early Church fathers encouraged praying for the dead from the very beginning – it was seen as an act of Christian charity, a way for those living to assist those dead but not yet in heaven. St. Augustine (beloved by Christians of all denominations), himself, said, "If we had no care for the dead, we would not be in the habit of praying for them."

Still, many non-Catholic Christians do not believe in Purgatory because they believe it has no basis in Scripture. However, there are several Biblical passages that support the doctrine of Purgatory.

It is true that the word "Purgatory" is not mentioned in Scripture. (Many theological terms that all Christians accept are not found in the Bible, either: "Trinity," for example.) The verb "purge" comes from a Latin term meaning "to purify." So Purgatory is a state of cleansing in which our souls are purified from sin.

The verb "purge" comes from a Latin term meaning "to purify." So Purgatory is a state of cleansing in which our souls are purified from sin.

In Revelation 21:27 it clearly states that, "nothing unclean will enter heaven." Likewise, in 1 Corinthians 3:15, St. Paul states that "if someone's work is burned up, that one will suffer loss; the person will be saved, but only as through fire." Clearly, the "fire" mentioned here by Paul cannot refer to hell because he says that the "person will be saved." There is no salvation for those in hell.

Jesus, Himself, teaches us that some sins can be forgiven in the "next world," as we hear in Matthew 12:32 and elsewhere (1 Peter 3:18-20, 4:6). St. Paul prayed for the dead, too (2 Timothy 1:16-18). In addition, there is a passage in 2 Maccabees 12:44-46 which clearly speaks of the existence of Purgatory. The real question, then, isn't "Where is Purgatory found in the Bible?" but "Why does there need to be a Purgatory at all?"

Christ accomplished our justification by dying on the cross. But the Bible teaches us that we are made holy over time (the process of sanctification), and this process involves suffering. Purgatory is just the final stage of sanctification for those in need of purification prior to entering the perfect and eternal banquet of heaven.

God is perfect holiness (Isaiah 6:3). We are called to be perfectly holy (Matthew 5:48; 1 Peter 1:15-16). Without perfect holiness, we cannot see God in heaven (Hebrews 12:14). Purgatory is meant for our cleansing and sanctification (Hebrews 12:11). All discipline and affliction leads us closer to God, if we let it (Romans 5:3-5; James 1:2).

Christ accomplished our justification by dying on the cross. But the Bible teaches us that we are made holy over time (the process of sanctification), and this process involves suffering. Purgatory is just the final stage of sanctification for those in need of purification prior to entering the perfect and eternal banquet of heaven.

One final thought – it's important to note that Purgatory is not a "second chance" for people who die in mortal sin. We must be vigilant in our pursuit for holiness, trying to avoid all sin – especially mortal sin – at all costs. Scripture differentiates between mortal (deadly) and venial sins (1 John 5:16-17; James 1:14-15). While mortal sin brings death to the soul (Romans 6:23), venial sin wounds the soul. To read more about the distinction on mortal and venial sin go to page 158.

Purgatory, too, is not something to "aim for." While many might jokingly say "I just want to make the cut for Purgatory" it's interesting to note that the saints who have been given visions of Purgatory don't describe it as a picnic, to say the least. We ought to be grateful to God for His great mercy, but at the same time, set our sights (and souls) on the higher goal of heaven.

SUGGESTED READING:
CCC 1030-36, 1472, 1861.
Cardinal Joseph Ratzinger (Pope Benedict XVI), *Eschatology*
Peter Kreeft, *Fundamentals of the Faith*

THE POPE

QUESTION 50

HOW CAN WE TRUST THE POPES WHEN SOME OF THEM HAVE BEEN VERY BAD?

IN BRIEF:

At the time of this book's publication, there have been 265 popes, and even though almost all of them have been incredible men, models of heroic virtue and deep holiness, there have absolutely been a handful of them over the centuries that were immoral, corrupt, and some downright nasty.

This might shock you. It does not shock many souls who are opposed to the Catholic Church or antagonistic toward the Church's authority. Some people believe if they can "expose" the so-called "bad popes" then it calls into question not only the legitimacy of the Papacy but also the reliability and overall truth of Church teachings.

But as the tortoise may have said to the hare, "Not so fast."

When Christ gave our first pope, St. Peter, the keys (Matthew 16:18-20) it wasn't as though Jesus thought (or said) that Peter would be "perfect" from that point on. Jesus knew Peter's sins even better than Peter did. In fact, just moments after calling Peter His "rock" (which you can read more about on page 202), Peter stuck his sandal in his mouth and Jesus rebuked him (Matthew 16:22-23)! Being entrusted with the responsibility of leading the Church didn't render any one of the 265 men perfect. They – like us - were all sinners...even the ones who were saints! The Pope goes to Reconciliation weekly (if not more). Personal sin did not keep anyone from being pope, not even the one Jesus, Himself, named. Personal sin also cannot inhibit the work or protection of the Holy Spirit (John 16:7-14). The protection of the Holy Spirit over the Church's teachings on faith and morals are higher than any person or person's power to govern.

Christ knew what He was doing when He entrusted the Spirit-guided Church to be led by sinners. You can't throw out the entire Church because of a few rotten members – that's not the Gospel. As one Catholic apologist put it, "You can't just leave Peter because of Judas."

IN DEPTH:

God's plans are higher than ours; His thoughts are far deeper and His perspective (obviously) perfect:

"For my thoughts are not your thoughts, neither are your ways my ways, says the LORD. For as the heavens are higher than the earth, so are my ways higher than your ways and my thoughts than your thoughts."

- Isaiah 55:8-9

Consider that Christ, Himself, not only picked Simon Peter the first pope as already discussed, but Judas Iscariot, as well. Did Jesus – the Son of God and Second Person of the Most Holy Trinity – make mistakes? Was He, perhaps, trying to teach us something?

What about Caiaphas, High Priest and pivotal character in Christ's wrongful conviction and ultimate death sentence? The Holy Spirit reminds us through the pen of St. John that even Caiaphas "uttered inspired prophecy" (John 11:49-55). God can use any sinner to ultimately accomplish His work of salvation. The manner in which God does it is not for us to know or comprehend (as Isaiah reminded us) but to trust in.

The notion that "if I can prove some popes have been immoral, then the teachings of the Catholic Church are false" is just plain silly. It's a disordered argument. The fact that there have been some immoral or wicked men who have sat in the pope's chair (a fact that Catholics don't deny) does not "disprove" the fact that Jesus instituted it nor render the reality of the Papacy any less important.

The fact that there have been some immoral or wicked men who have sat in the pope's chair (a fact that Catholics don't deny) does not "disprove" the fact that Jesus instituted it nor render the reality of the Papacy any less important.

Does weakness disqualify any Christian from service? Are any of us – even those of us who are devoted followers, prayer warriors, or daily Mass-goers – not weak? Are we not all in constant need of God's mercy? St. Paul not only admitted his weakness, he *boasted* of it (1 Corinthians 1:26-29). Isn't God's grace ultimately far more powerful than our sin (Romans 6:1-2)?

St. Paul goes on to remind us that St. Peter – though imperfect

– was the apostle all sought out for guidance (Galatians 1:18-19). St. Paul, himself, though he argues with St. Peter, also submits to his ultimate authority. One of the greatest dangers of spending so much time and energy focusing on the handful that were wicked is missing out on the 97 percent of the popes who were so incredibly good! How about Linus, Cletus, Clement, Sixtus I, Cornelius, and Fabian (just to name a few) leading through times of intense persecution? They spent most of their Pontificates standing up to Emperors or staring down a ferocious beast waiting to devour them.

Following Peter's martyrdom the popes were not only known as the Bishops of Rome but as "Successors of Peter," demonstrating the unbroken lineage between Peter and our current Holy Father.

Whether one of the very rare sinners or the overwhelming number of saints, one thing every pope had in common is that they are (were) Peter. Just like the original Peter, when they take their eyes off of Christ, they sink (Matthew 14:30). When humble enough to seek Christ for their safety and salvation, Jesus always responds. Following Peter's martyrdom the popes were not only known as the Bishops of Rome but as "Successors of Peter," demonstrating the unbroken lineage between Peter and our current Holy Father.

While some have made mistakes the Holy Spirit has continued to protect us. Our popes have ended wars, converted countries, saved civilizations, and brought down walls (quite literally, as seen with Blessed John Paul II in communist Europe). The Church and the world are far better off with popes than without them, beyond any doubt.

Oh, and for those who are still more worried about the three percent of immoral men who have led the universal Church than the 97 percent of saintly popes, remind them that any popes who did not faithfully live out their Baptismal call to virtue or who were not faithful to the blessings and grace God gave them were (and will ultimately be) dealt with in God's justice.

Let us never forget the heroism of the majority.

SUGGESTED READING:
Patrick Madrid, *Pope Fiction*

IS EVERYTHING THE POPE SAYS INFALLIBLE?

IN BRIEF:

If so, I'd like to follow him in to buy a lottery ticket. Sadly, that's not going to help my chances, for a variety of reasons.

First, the word "infallible" means incapable of making mistakes. People use the phrase "infallible" way too liberally when speaking about the Church. No, the pope is not always infallible; he is human. He is not a fortuneteller, a psychic, or an illusionist. He may be a prophet, however, and he is definitely an apostle.

Second, infallibility only pertains to matters of faith and morals. You will never see an infallible statement come out of the Vatican about a sports team, game, or match, nor about what music group is best or what candidate is strongest. The Vatican, likewise, does not issue infallible statements on the economy, the future, or people. Again, infallibility has to do with faith and morals only.

Lastly, even when the Church makes a statement about something pertaining to faith and morals, for any statement to be deemed "infallible," the pope needs to be speaking *ex cathedra* or "from the chair." It means that the doctrine in question has been officially taught from the chair of Peter to the entire world and that, as such, the pope (as the universal shepherd) in agreement with the Magisterium is preserved from error through the power of the Holy Spirit, who guides, protects, and empowers Mother Church. Just a brief side note here, too: he doesn't "literally" have to be sitting in the chair to make an ex cathedra statement.

IN DEPTH:

Some people think the Church is egotistical to claim anything as irrefutable truth or to declare any moral doctrine infallible. Such is the sad result of living in a moral relativist culture that refuses to believe in or acknowledge absolute truth. In reality, the concept of authority is lost on them, but it was not lost on Christ.

It might interest you to know that in the entire 2000 years of Catholic history, there have only been two specific *ex cathedra* statements:

- Pope Pius IX defined the Immaculate Conception on December 8, 1854.

- Pope Pius XII defined the Assumption of Mary on November 1, 1950.

There have been other times that teachings were deemed infallible, such as the ongoing teaching that abortion is inherently evil and wrong. While that teaching did not come *ex cathedra*, it has (obviously) always been consistently taught as infallible and will continue to be.

These instances are explained in more detail in *Lumen Gentium*:

> *"This loyal submission of the will and intellect must be given, in a special way, to the authentic authority of the Roman pontiff, even when he does not speak ex cathedra, in such wise, indeed, that his supreme teaching authority be acknowledged with respect and sincere assent be given to decisions made by him."*
>
> *- Lumen Gentium, 25*

Christ acknowledged the authority of an Old Testament Magisterium (Matthew 23:2-3) during His earthly ministry, and in giving Peter the keys (Matthew 16:18-19), Christ did not only establish a New Testament Magisterium, but also respected the prime minister role as accentuated centuries before (Isaiah 22:20-25). In fact, when Jesus Christ empowered His apostles with the ability "to bind and loose," He was ensuring that such an infallible authority and structure would persist long after His Ascension (John 14:16, 16:13; Matthew 28:20). The pope and, indeed, the fullness of the Magisterium, are empowered with the apostolic authority of Christ (Matthew 10:40; Luke 10:16; 2 Corinthians 5:18-20) still today.

There have been other times that teachings were deemed infallible, such as the ongoing teaching that abortion is inherently evil and wrong. While that teaching did not come ex cathedra, it has (obviously) always been consistently taught as infallible and will continue to be.

In the First Vatican Council (1870), papal infallibility was more formally explained as follows:

"We teach and define that it is a dogma Divinely revealed: that the Roman pontiff, when he speaks ex cathedra — that is, when in discharge of the office of Pastor and Doctor of all Christians, by virtue of his supreme apostolic authority, he defines a doctrine regarding faith or morals to be held by the universal Church, by the Divine assistance promised to him in blessed Peter — is possessed of that infallibility with which the Divine Redeemer willed that His Church should be endowed in defining doctrine regarding faith or morals; and that therefore such definitions of the Roman pontiff are irreformable of themselves and not from the consent of the Church."

When Jesus Christ empowered His apostles with the ability "to bind and loose," He was ensuring that such an infallible authority and structure would persist long after His Ascension.

- Constitutio de Ecclesiâ Christi

SUGGESTED READING:
CCC 85-88, 95, 888-892, 2032-2036
Patrick Madrid, *Pope Fiction*
The Staff of Catholic Answers, *The Essential Catholic Survival Guide*

WHY DO WE HAVE A POPE? IS IT REALLY BIBLICAL?

IN BRIEF:

Every company needs a President or CEO, someone to give it a guiding vision and pass that vision on to the people in the company. A good CEO points out where a company needs to improve in order to fulfill the mission given to it by the founder.

Jesus had countless souls who learned from Him but only 72 of His followers were empowered to preach and heal during His earthly ministry (prior to the crucifixion). Out of those 72, He had twelve who He worked with quite intimately. They were sent out on a very specific apostolic mission (apostle means "one who is sent") after being trained by Christ, Himself. Out of those twelve, there were three that He selected to be in His closest, inner circle of friends: Peter, James, and John. These facts are all Biblically proven – you can read about them all.

Each of the three was given a special role in the Church. Peter was the "rock" on which Jesus would build His Church (Matthew 16:18-19). As every group needs a leader, someone to cast the deciding vote, so did the apostles and the bishops. Simon Peter, the fisherman, rose to the occasion. In his line are popes who became saints and popes who were less than saintly; yet every pope was given special authority by God to guide the Church for a time.

IN DEPTH:

So, "why would Jesus entrust His Church to humans...to sinners?" one might ask.

It's not like Jesus didn't know that people were going to sin; He knows all—He's God. The Church, like Jesus Christ, is both human and divine. So while the Church is *divinely* fueled, guided by the Holy Spirit, and perfect in her teachings, it is still composed of humans who are imperfect. Sin exists in the pews just as much as it does in the sacristies and even when people in leadership sin, that does not render God's laws or God's truths any less valid or truthful.

Christ knew (Simon) Peter was not perfect; yet He still chose him for an all-important task of guiding the Church on earth:

> *"And so I say to you (Simon), you are Peter, and upon this rock I will build my church, and the gates of the netherworld shall not prevail against it. I will give you the keys to the kingdom of heaven. Whatever you bind on earth shall be bound in heaven; and whatever you loose on earth shall be loosed in heaven."*
>
> *- Matthew 16:18-19*

Notice that Jesus essentially does five things here:

- Jesus changes Simon's name to Peter.

- Jesus tells Peter that He is going to build His Church upon him.

- Jesus promises that "the netherworld" will not prevail against the Church.

- Jesus gives Peter "the keys."

- Jesus gives Peter the power "to bind" and "to loose."

Let's deal with each one briefly, in terms that we can understand:

Jesus changes Simon's name to Peter.

This is a big deal because only God can change a name. Why is it a big deal? Because a change in someone's name signals a change in a person's essence. While "rock" was used to speak about God (and even Abraham) in the Old Testament, Peter is the only person to be designated "the rock" by Christ. When the New Testament writers were translating Jesus' Aramaic to Koine Greek, they were quite intentional and careful about how to phrase this exactly, so as not to lose the proper, intended meaning (Koine is a specific dialect). The exact wording for "rock" between the Aramaic *"kepha"* and the Greek *"petros/petra"* is something amateur Bible enthusiasts try to use against the Catholic Church, but a closer understanding of how the different languages transliterate masculine and feminine pronouns quickly dismisses supposed inconsistencies and prove, clearly, that the Catholic Church did – and does – have its feet firmly planted "on the rock" of truth. Besides, if Jesus was not

The Church, like Jesus Christ, is both human and divine. So while the Church is divinely fueled, guided by the Holy Spirit, and perfect in her teachings, it is still composed of humans who are imperfect.

doing something important here and in essence setting Simon apart, why change the name?

To be clear, this designation did not mean that Peter became divine, but let's say that it carries with it a "divine assistance" – an assistance that Jesus promises us (Matthew 28:20, John 16:7).

Jesus tells Peter that He is going to build His Church (upon him).

While that is a pretty straightforward statement, some people believe that the first time Jesus says "rock" that He is referring to Peter, and the second time He says it, that He's referring to Himself. Not a bad idea but shortsighted for a lot of reasons (again, dealing with Greek translations). Besides, Peter is living in Christ and Christ in Peter, so that doesn't really pose a problem.

> *To be clear, this designation did not mean that Peter became divine, but let's say that it carries with it a "divine assistance" – an assistance that Jesus promises us (Matthew 28:20, John 16:7).*

Jesus promises that "the netherworld" will not prevail against the Church.

Okay, so what will evil never prevail against? The Church. People point to modern problems within the Church or a scandal as some sort of proof that Christ was talking about Himself as the Church, not a Church on Earth. Not true. Battles may be lost, but never the war. The Church will always prevail – Christ promises us that.

Jesus gives Peter "the keys."

You know this one: when you turn sixteen, and you're with your friends going out, who is the one in control? The one with the car keys. The person with the keys is in the driver's seat (literally), and nothing has changed in two thousand years. The keys not only let people in, they lock people out. The keys signify power. This action, too, is Biblical. As seen in Isaiah 22, the Prime Minister of Israel is given the keys, and with that, the power to govern God's people on earth. What Jesus was doing was not only landmark for the future, but also rooted in the past.

Think about what it says in Luke 10:16, "Whoever listens to you listens to me. Whoever rejects you rejects me. And whoever rejects me rejects the one who sent me." The one driving is the one who steers where the car is going. The other passengers can object (reject), but they weren't given the keys, and thus, can't steer. None of the other apostles get the keys, nor do any of the other New Testament figures...think about it.

Jesus gives Peter the power "to bind" and "to loose." What does that mean? Sacramental power through Confession and Reconciliation. Ask yourself, how would Peter, the apostles, or any priest know which sins "to bind" or "to loose" if they had not heard the sins, first. And Jesus is very clear; they have authority on earth that counts in heaven.

Finally, if people say that Peter was nothing special, there are several Scriptural episodes beyond the truths laid out here to counteract such a ridiculous claim:

- Peter's name appears first in every Scriptural listing of the names of the apostles (Matthew 10:2-4; Mark 3:16-19; Luke 6:12-19; Acts 1:13). In fact, take note of how St. Matthew writes it under the Holy Spirit's inspiration, "The names of the twelve apostles are these: ***first***, Simon called Peter, and his brother Andrew; James, the son of Zebedee, and his brother John... (Matthew 10:2, emphasis added). The word "first" in Greek reads (*protos*) which means "the best" or "the foremost." Words matter.

- Peter was the first apostle to whom Christ appeared after His Resurrection (Luke 24:34 and 1 Corinthians 15:5).

- Peter is singled out by the angels (Mark 16:7).

- Peter is the only apostle for whom Christ personally prayed and then commissioned (Luke 22:31-32).

- Peter is only one given the charge as pastor to "feed the sheep" (John 21:15-17).

- Peter oversees the election of the apostle to take Judas Iscariot's place (Acts 1:15-26).

- Peter receives the revelation to welcome Gentiles (non-Jews) into the Church (Acts 10:9-49).

- Peter becomes the spokesperson for the Apostles on serious matters (Mark 8:29; John 6:68-69; Acts 2:14-41).

- Peter is the one who defends the Christian Church against the Jewish Sanhedrin (Acts chapters 4 and 15).

- Peter is the first one to perform a miracle in Jesus' name following the descent of the Holy Spirit at Pentecost (Acts 3:1-10).

Even St. Paul, the author of half the New Testament and arguably the greatest missionary the world has ever known, shows his obedience to Peter in his letter to the Galatians (Galatians 1:18), and it's no secret that Peter and Paul had major differences in opinion at times.

Even St. Paul, the author of half the New Testament and arguably the greatest missionary the world has ever known, shows his obedience to Peter in his letter to the Galatians (Galatians 1:18).

Since Peter was martyred, we have been blessed with an unbroken apostolic succession; that is why we have had a successor to the chair of Peter ever since his crucifixion in the mid-first century. Some claim that the Church, at times, had "multiple popes." That is not true. At certain times there have been more than one person "claiming" to be the Pontiff. However, there has only been one *true pope* at a time.

The Papacy is not only rooted in Scripture, it is safeguarded by Scripture's Author: the Holy Spirit.

SUGGESTED READING:

CCC 891-92, 100, 882
Patrick Madrid, *Pope Fiction*
The Staff of Catholic Answers, *The Essential Catholic Survival Guide*
Fr. Mario Romero, *Unabridged Christianity*

MARY AND THE SAINTS

WHY DO CATHOLICS BELIEVE IN THE IMMACULATE CONCEPTION?

IN BRIEF:

Think about this for a minute. Why would the Catholic Church, in the middle of Advent and Christmas preparation, pause to celebrate the Immaculate Conception – yet another holy day – on December 8th?

Why pause to honor Mary while we're prepping to party with Jesus? What is the Immaculate Conception, and why is it a big deal?

God was hoping you would ask.

First, we need to be clear here. **The Immaculate Conception is not about the conception of Jesus in Mary's womb. It's about the conception of Mary in her mother's womb years before.**

While Mary was conceived in the normal, human way through her parents (Joachim and Anne), the Immaculate Conception speaks to the fact that Mary was conceived without the stain of original sin. Immaculate literally means "without stain."

IN DEPTH:

So why would God preserve Mary from original sin? The Blessed Virgin Mary was conceived without original sin in order to preserve her as the perfect vessel through which our Lord would become flesh to the world. This does not mean, however, that Mary was not in need of a Savior. Jesus redeemed Mary, too, but in a unique way.

You and I are conceived with the stain of original sin (unleashed in Eden by our ancestors Adam and Eve), and we need Baptism to wash away that stain and cleanse our souls.

The difference is that when Mary was conceived, God intervened and chose to prevent Mary's soul from bearing that stain.

Now, this is where some Christians point to Romans 3:23, which clearly states: "All have sinned and fall short of the glory of God, they are justified by His grace as a gift, through the redemption which is in Christ Jesus."

And as I mentioned earlier, Mary, herself, proclaims God as her "Savior" (Luke 1:47). The Catholic Church absolutely agrees with this fact and teaches (in *Lumen Gentium*, 53 – 56) exactly how Mary "was redeemed by the merits of her Son" (*CCC* 492).

One could say that Mary's redemption was proactive; while Christ's sacrifice removes our sin, it *preserved* Mary from it.

I know – this is deep stuff.

Picture it like this: you're walking down a path in the forest and you fall into a deep, dark pit. That pit represents original sin. Someone reaches in to pull you out; they are now your "savior." In Mary's case, before she fell into the pit, God intervened and lifted her over it. He preserved her from the pain (and the stain). This was also a form of saving her – just in a different way.

The difference is that when Mary was conceived, God intervened and chose to prevent Mary's soul from bearing that stain.

Even the saints wrestled to get their heads around this truth. St. Augustine, for example, believed it and proclaimed it. St. Thomas Aquinas struggled with it, fearing that it implied that Mary didn't need a Savior. Over time, however, his continued prayer and humility gave way to a deeper understanding of this truth and its Scriptural roots.

More Than a Woman.
Remember what the angel said when he greeted Mary in the Gospel of Luke, "Rejoice, O highly favored daughter!" (Luke 1:28). The better, more accurate translation reads, "Rejoice, you who are full of grace!" (from the Greek phrase *kecharitomene*).

Without getting too deep into Greek here, it's important to note that the term indicates that Mary was "graced" already (not by the angel's visit), and that she still was (at that point) filled with a superabundance of God's grace. The Greek speaks to her character and quality, not her "luck." This was not an announcement that Mary had randomly won some divine lottery.

She had been set apart – chosen and preserved – from the beginning of time.

This means that God prepared Mary to be clean (sinless) so that she could give birth to the Son of God. This doesn't mean that she was never tempted. She was. The Church says that she was filled with the love of the Holy Spirit, and that there was no room for sin to take over. That's a lot of love.

If you want to read more about this teaching, check out the *Catechism of the Catholic Church*, paragraphs 721 – 726.

Did the Church Just Make This Up?

Because the doctrine of the Immaculate Conception wasn't officially defined until 1854, some think that means that the Catholic Church just made it up. What people have to remember, however, is that this doesn't mean it wasn't *believed* or *taught* prior to that. *It was.*

You see, the Church is pretty busy defending truth and offering a billion souls the Sacraments. She doesn't usually stop to "officially define" an understood doctrine unless there is some controversy or need for clarification. Sometimes, though, the Church officially declares a long-understood truth because it helps the faithful to grow even more deeply in understanding and devotion (which is the case here). The Pope saw the need for Mary's intercession even more greatly in the modernizing Church and he wanted to encourage deeper prayer and devotion to her intercession.

Ask Yourself.

"Wouldn't God, in His infinite wisdom, want the body and womb that carried Christ to be a perfect and pure dwelling place?"

"Why wouldn't God want to set apart the woman who would give birth to His only Son?"

"Wouldn't the same God who rose a star in the sky as a heavenly birth announcement to earth (Matthew 2:2), who emptied Himself and took on flesh (Philippians 2:7), and who conquered death and rose from the dead (Acts 2:24; Romans 6:9) be willing to go above and beyond in this way, too?"

Wouldn't God want Mary to be a stainless vessel and a model of perfect discipleship to carry and raise His only Son, Jesus?

Sounds like the perfect plan from our perfect God who is perfect Love (Matthew 5:48, 1 John 4:18).

SUGGESTED READING:
CCC 490-93
Fulton Sheen, *The World's First Love*
Scott Hahn, *Hail Holy Queen: The Mother of God in the Word of God*
Pope Benedict XVI, Mary: *The Church at the Source*

DO CATHOLICS WORSHIP MARY?
WHY NOT JUST FOCUS ON JESUS?

IN BRIEF:

This is one of the most popular misconceptions when it comes to the Catholic faith. No Church on earth celebrates and honors the Blessed Virgin Mary like the Catholic Church does, to be sure.

Remember during the Visitation Mary says, "[...] henceforth all generations will call me blessed" (Luke 1:48). That was not an egocentric proclamation; Mary's not looking for props, she's not exalting herself above anyone. Mary's proclamation was a prophecy, and we are living out that prophecy to the highest extent. When we honor Mary, we are following God's example of honoring her and setting her apart. After all, if Jesus hadn't honored His mother, He would have violated the Fourth Commandment! Honoring Mary doesn't take anything away from our love for God – not in the slightest.

Consider it this way: you've seen a football player score a touchdown and celebrate, and when the camera zooms in on him sitting on the bench after, he looks straight into the camera and says, "Hi, Mom!" That very public act of love and affirmation of his mother isn't taken to mean the player doesn't love his father. Most people would agree that we have "different" relationships with our mothers and fathers – not loving one more than the other, but it's slightly different in how we approach them and what we seek them for.

> *We don't adore Mary; we venerate her ("venerate" comes from a Latin word meaning "to revere or respect").*

IN DEPTH:

No, Catholics do not worship Mary; we worship God and God, alone. We do honor Mary, however, and offer her the praise she deserves (as exemplified above). We *adore* God (like we do in Adoration of the Blessed Sacrament). We don't adore Mary; we *venerate* her ("venerate" comes from a Latin word meaning "to revere or respect"). We will discuss the difference between praying *with* her and praying *to* her in the following section on praying with saints.

God obviously exalted Mary above any other creature – as evidenced through her Immaculate Conception and her glorious Assumption (both of which we'll explain in further detail). It is interesting to note, too, that when the angel Gabriel addresses the Blessed Virgin "Hail, oh favored one [...]" (Luke 1:28) that it is the only time in all of the Sacred Scriptures that an angel – a messenger of God – refers to someone as a title rather than their name.

In honoring Mary we are actually being quite Scriptural. God constantly repeats the command to "honor your father and mother" (Exodus 20:12; Leviticus 19:3; Deuteronomy 5:16; Matthew 15:4; Ephesians 6:2). Likewise, we are encouraged to show honor to those in authority (Matthew 10:41; Romans 13:7; Ephesians 6:5; 1 Timothy 5:17, 6:1; 1 Peter 2:17). In honoring Mary – who was given to us as our spiritual mother (John 19:26-27) – we follow in Christ's footsteps and fulfill God's command.

Mary is the new Eve, perfectly obedient and mother to all the living. Christ proves this by calling Mary "woman" at Cana (John 2) and upon the cross (John 19). This was not a sign of disrespect (since Jesus is sinless – Hebrews 4:16) but, rather, to demonstrate that Mary fulfills the first prophecy we hear of in Genesis 3:15. Christ is the New Adam, setting straight (in the garden of Gethsemane and the Easter tomb) what went wrong in the Garden of Eden. Mary is the new Eve; her faithful "yes" helps "undo" what was done in the beginning with the serpent (Genesis 3).

Mary is not an "addition" within Catholic beliefs; it's more like Mary is Catholicism. She is the perfect disciple. She is everything we are called to be. While we'll never be perfect like Mary, our pursuit of Christ should lead us to saintliness like hers: rooted in humility, trust, service, and love.

Why Not Just Focus Only on Jesus?
A popular question from people, especially non-Catholics, is, "Why focus at all on Mary? Why not just focus on Jesus?" Often, the question is asked with sincere intentions, but stems from an erroneous idea that Catholics take their attention off of Jesus to focus on Mary. At no time has the Catholic Church ever suggested taking the attention or focus off of Christ. We, as Catholics and Christians, are encouraged, implored, and commanded to look to Christ and focus on Him in our prayers.

The misunderstanding comes in when people think that Mary takes the place of Christ, which she does not. Nor does our invitation to Mary to pray for us get in the way of Christ praying to God on our behalf. Mary doesn't get in the way of Christ being our mediator to God. She enhances it.

When we pray, we invite Mary to join her prayers to ours, praying with us to Christ. Mary does not **and would not** do anything to divert the glory away from Jesus. She lived to glorify God. Anyone who disagrees should read **Luke 1:46-56**.

At no time has the Catholic Church ever suggested taking the attention or focus off of Christ. We, as Catholics and Christians, are encouraged, implored, and commanded to look to Christ and focus on Him in our prayers.

A few things I share with or ask people who pose this question to me:

• When Mary came to Christ with a need (John 2) did He respond to her? Yes.

• Did Jesus hold Mary in high esteem, honoring her like a Son should? Yes.

• Did Jesus give her to us as a mother (John 19)? Yes.

•Did Mary hold a place of honor in the early Church (Acts 1-2)? Yes.

It tells us in Scripture (Galatians 2:20) that we become "little Christs" when we follow Him. We are called to imitate Christ in every way (1 Corinthians 11:1). We must seek to be just like Jesus. In prayer, ask Christ to grant you His Heart in every way.

Pray:

I want to have the heart for God that you have, Jesus.
I want to have the heart for the poor that you have, Jesus.
I want to have the heart for sinners that you have, Jesus.
I want to have the heart for the Word that you have, Jesus.
I want to have the heart of mercy that you have, Jesus.
I want to have the heart for Your Mother that you have, Jesus.

I have yet to find someone who truly prays that prayer who does not hold Mary in the beautiful esteem that she, as the Mother of God, deserves. She will hold you and walk with you, whenever you call upon her. She is always directing your path perfectly and gently back to her Son...like a good mother does.

SUGGESTED READING:

CCC 971, 2675-79
Frank Sheed, *Theology for Beginners*
Fulton Sheen, *The World's First Love*
Scott Hahn, Hail Holy Queen: *The Mother of God in the Word of God*
Pope Benedict XVI, Mary: *The Church at the Source*

WHAT IF MARY WOULD HAVE SAID "NO"?

IN BRIEF:

Well, if Mary had said "no" we would save a lot of money on Christmas shopping, and the world would have a one-way ticket to hell.

Seriously, though, before answering this question, it is necessary to assess why the person is asking it. Are they a sincere believer in Christ and loyal to Christ's Church just unleashing their "theological imagination," or is there a deeper strategy at play?

Questions such as these are sometimes brought up to try to "trap" someone into saying that Mary didn't have free will, or that God is some sort of sadistic "puppet master" type who forces people to do His bidding.

To be clear, Mary could have said "no" because she had free will. That being said, given her sinlessness (as a result of her Immaculate Conception), it would not have been within her nature to say no or to do anything that would not be in line with the will of God.

IN DEPTH:

Some might argue that if Mary had said no, God would have just chosen someone else who would have said yes. While God is omnipotent and omniscient and can, quite obviously, do whatever He wants, that argument doesn't really stack up logically.

It is vital to note that just because God knew that she would say "yes" does not impinge upon her free will.

God set the plan for the preservation of Mary in action eternally before the angel Gabriel visited her on that one fine day in Nazareth (this event is known as the "Annunciation" - read Luke 1, again, if you haven't in a while).

God created and formed Mary in the womb with great care (just as He does with each of us – check out Psalm 139:13-16). She was free to say "no" at that moment in time, but she didn't; besides, God exists above and beyond time. He is utterly timeless.

It is vital to note that just because God knew that she would say "yes" does not impinge upon her free will. In a very basic sense, take this as an example of how God's knowledge of Mary's willingness and answer did not take her free will away from her:

Say "Tim" goes over to his parents' house and upon entering and greeting them, he proceeds to the kitchen where he opens the refrigerator. Upon opening the door, Tim notices that there are only two things to eat: a plate of chocolate cake and a plate of liver. Now, Tim's father and mother know which one he's going to choose. Their knowledge of his choice, however, has nothing to do with Tim's choice, and in no way strips him of his free will to choose either one.

Get it?

You know what's even more impressive for us as modern day Catholics?

Rather than spending too much time focusing on the "what ifs" surrounding the Annunciation, grab your rosary and celebrate the "what did" happen.

In her **yes** response (called the "fiat") we have the greatest and most beautiful example of discipleship, humility, acceptance, praise, and worship ever uttered from human lips: "Behold, I am a handmaid of the Lord, may it be done to me according to thy Word " (Luke 1:38).

Rather than spending too much time focusing on the "what ifs" surrounding the Annunciation, grab your rosary and celebrate the "what did" happen.

SUGGESTED READING:
Fulton Sheen, *The World's First Love*
Scott Hahn, *Hail Holy Queen: The Mother of God in the Word of God*
Pope Benedict XVI, *Mary: The Church at the Source*

DID MARY HAVE OTHER CHILDREN AFTER JESUS?

IN BRIEF:

A funnier question than "Did Mary have other children?" would have been "If Jesus had brothers, would he have fought with them over toys?" Just kidding, Jesus wouldn't fight; He would just multiply the toys so every sibling had their own. Again, kidding.

To be clear, the Catholic Church teaches – and has always taught – that Mary, the Mother of Jesus, was a perpetual virgin. She never had sexual relations with Joseph, not even after Jesus' birth.

In passages that speak about Jesus' "brethren" or "brothers" (like in Luke 8:19), it may seem like the verse is implying that Mary and Joseph had children after Jesus' birth; this wasn't the case. St. Jerome made it a point to distinguish that the word "brethren" could refer not only to actual blood-related 'brothers,' but also to extended family, like cousins. The New Testament was originally written in Greek, and the Greek word for brother, *adelphos* (like many Greek words), has many meanings. It could include almost any male relative you were related to, not only by blood, but even by marriage. The term "brother" could also refer to close friends or "kinsmen."

Finally, it's also interesting to keep in mind that no word existed in Hebrew or Aramaic (the language that Jesus spoke daily) for 'cousin.'

IN DEPTH:

The idea that Mary "must have had sexual relations" based on Scripture is – ironically – a poor reading of Scripture.

Take the most "popular" verse used to say that Mary did not remain a virgin: "When Joseph woke from sleep, he did as the angel of the Lord commanded him; he took his wife, but knew her not until she had borne a son; and he called His name Jesus" (Matthew 1:24-25). Not to go real heavy into the original Greek of that verse, but the actual Greek used for "until" is *heos hou*, which can be read as "before" or "until" but neither reading in the Greek implies that "after Jesus was born" Mary and Joseph had sex. That's not what the phrase reads. It reads that they did not have sex to ensure that the readers and hearers of the Gospel would know there was no way that Jesus was Joseph's biological son.

St. Matthew put it there, through the inspiration of the Holy Spirit, to ensure that there were no misunderstandings. And it's not just Catholics who "read it this way." It is an ecumenical (multiple different faith denominations) truth that the finest Biblical theologians and scholars attested to for decades. To suggest that "until" means that they must have had sexual relations or more children after Jesus' birth isn't common sense or good attention, it's poor exegesis (which we discussed in the "In Brief" section on page 90). Don't be afraid to crack open the *Catechism* on this one, either (CCC 496-501, 510) and read specifically what the Catholic Church teaches.

> To suggest that "until" means that they must have had sexual relations or more children after Jesus' birth isn't common sense or good attention, it's poor exegesis.

Well, then what about Jesus' "other" brothers, isn't that enough proof?

Sometimes people fall into the trap that because their Bible occasionally refers to the "brothers of Jesus" (Mark 3:31-32; John 7:3-10) that Mary must have had other kids following Christ. Again, the translation is an important issue.

- Realize that the Greek language is not like the English that you speak. The word "brothers" in these translations encompasses far more than "blood brothers." It includes (but is not limited to) stepbrothers, adopted brothers, cousins, close family friends, and (in some cases) even the children of handmaids or servants.

- The "brothers of Jesus," James and Joseph, are sons of another Mary whom St. Matthew called the other Mary (Matthew 28:1; *CCC* 500). She is known as the wife of Clopas; he is believed to be St. Joseph's brother.

- Many scholars believe that the "brothers" are sons of St. Joseph from a previous marriage, thus, making them stepbrothers. This idea of Joseph as a widower is hotly contested among certain saints and theologians.

- For the first 1600 years or so (until the Protestant Reformation), it was a commonly held belief that Mary was a perpetual virgin. This goes to show not the Church's dominance in thought, but the commonly held Tradition passed down from generation to generation, especially among St. John and his followers (the Johannine community) with whom Mary lived following the Passion of our Lord (John 19:27), according to Tradition.

Some Christians might wonder, "Does all this really matter?"

Mary's perpetual virginity matters on several levels. There is a lot to learn from this truth. It says a lot about her, about Joseph, about God, about the Church, about our modern society, and about our call to holiness.

The Church celebrates the Blessed Virgin Mary and her perpetual sacrifice calling Her Aeiparthenos or "Ever Virgin" (*CCC* 499; *Lumen Gentium*, 52). The Church honors Joseph as the patron saint of chastity for his self-control and self-sacrificing nature. In this modern culture, when we are told that to deny our own sexual urges is wrong or "unnatural," we are reminded of two courageous young souls who thought more of God than of one another. Whether married, single, or celibate this is a great example to both genders on the beauty of chastity, self-sacrifice, and finding our ultimate joy and peace in God and not in one another. Today's culture teaches that "within marriage, everything is okay" but that can quickly lead to people having and using their spouses for sex and (at times) very selfish, personal fulfillment only – contraceptives work toward that very disordered purpose.

The Church celebrates the Blessed Virgin Mary and her perpetual sacrifice calling Her Aeiparthenos or "Ever Virgin" (CCC 499; Lumen Gentium, 52).

Mary totally consecrated herself to God (as Sacred Tradition affirms). She had respect for the fact that God – perfect and undefiled – had dwelt within her womb. What other human child would be worthy of sharing that dignity within her womb? How and why would sin be allowed within her, through Joseph? Her call to be the Mother of Jesus proves and solidifies her call to be the Mother of all Christians, since Jesus is, absolutely, our brother and Lord.

Honestly, it's not like Mary was "missing out." One can only imagine what an amazing and intense reality it would be to have the Holy Spirit so profoundly within you that you conceive a child. Bearing that in mind, what need would Mary have for a human concept or experience of conception following that reality? None, really; it would just be a matter of self-control on both her and Joseph's part.

It's important to note that Mary's perpetual virginity is intimately tied to her Immaculate Conception, which is a different answer, as well, but worth reading more about on page 210.

There are several saints who commented on this doctrine, whose writings and teachings are held in high esteem among all Christians, both Catholics and Protestants alike:

As St. Jerome put it:

> "The brethren of the Lord not as being sons of Mary but brethren in the sense I have explained, that is to say, brethren in point of kinship, not by nature. [By discussing such things we] are [...] following the tiny streams of opinion. Might I not array against you the whole series of ancient writers? Ignatius, Polycarp, Irenaeus, Justin Martyr, and many other apostolic and eloquent men, who against [the heretics] Ebion, Theodotus of Byzantium, and Valentinus, held these same views and wrote volumes replete with wisdom. If you had ever read what they wrote, you would be a wiser man."
> - Against Helvidius: The Perpetual Virginity of Mary 19 [A.D. 383]

As St. Augustine put it:

> "In being born of a Virgin who chose to remain a Virgin even before she knew who was to be born of her, Christ wanted to approve virginity rather than to impose it. And He wanted virginity to be of free choice even in that woman in whom He took upon Himself the form of a slave."
> - Holy Virginity 4:4 [A.D. 401]

> "It was not the visible sun, but its invisible Creator who consecrated this day for us, when the Virgin Mother, fertile of womb and integral in her virginity, brought Him forth, made visible for us, by whom, when He was invisible, she too was created. A Virgin conceiving, a Virgin bearing, a Virgin pregnant, a Virgin bringing forth, a Virgin perpetual. Why do you wonder at this, O man?"
> - Sermons 186:1 [A.D. 411]

"Heretics called Antidicomarites are those who contradict the perpetual virginity of Mary and affirm that after Christ was born she was joined as one with her husband."

- Heresies 56 [A.D. 428]

As Origen put it:

"The power from on high overshadowed her. And I think it in harmony with reason that Jesus was the firstfruit among men of the purity which consists in [perpetual] chastity, and Mary was among women. For it were not pious to ascribe to any other than to her the firstfruit of virginity."

- Commentary on Matthew 2:17 [A.D. 248]

As St. Cyril of Alexandria put it:

"The Word Himself, coming into the Blessed Virgin herself, assumed for Himself His own temple from the substance of the Virgin and came forth from her a man in all that could be externally discerned, while interiorly He was true God. Therefore He kept His Mother a virgin even after her childbearing."

- Against Those Who Do Not Wish to Confess That the Holy Virgin is the Mother of God [A.D. 430]

SUGGESTED READING:

CCC 496-507
The Staff of Catholic Answers, *The Essential Catholic Survival Guide*
Fulton Sheen, *The World's First Love*
Scott Hahn, *Hail Holy Queen: The Mother of God in the Word of God*

IS IT WRONG TO PRAY TO THE SAINTS?

IN BRIEF:

It's important to explain that there are different types of prayer. Prayer can be petitionary, intercessory, adoration, praise, thanksgiving, etc. These different types of prayer can be used at different times of your spiritual walk – they all have the same intention of growing our relationship with God and helping us to grow in His grace – but they are different "routes" to the same destination.

To be clear, prayer to God includes worship. Prayer with Mary and the saints includes honor, but not worship. We are always going to God. Always. Sometimes, however, we ask others to come along on our journey to God. Like Dorothy heading to see the Wizard, it's good to have friends along for the ride – friends (like the saints) who know the lay of the land...after all, Oz isn't the only place with "streets of gold" (Revelation 21:21).

IN DEPTH:

Just to make it very clear up front, Catholics and Protestants believe firmly in the command that we are to pray to God constantly, and without reservation (1 Thessalonians 5:16-17). We agree on that.

The Catholic Church does not and has never encouraged people to take their attention or prayer off of or away from Jesus.

> **The Catholic Church does not and has never encouraged people to take their attention or prayer off of or away from Jesus.**

When a friend of yours prays for you, it's called secondary mediation. When you ask for prayers from a saint, you are doing the same thing and they are joining their prayers to your own, en route to Christ. Since they're closer to Him than you are, it actually makes more sense for them to pray for you than for your earthly friends to do so.

Mediation.

Many people are confused about what "mediation" really is and quote something like 1 Timothy 2:5 – speaking about how Christ is the only Mediator between man and God (which the Catholic Church agrees with, by the way).

But mediation, in a more general sense, is any one of us praying for or with each other. This is what St. Paul encourages in the four verses immediately preceding that verse about Christ as the one Mediator (1 Timothy 2:1-4).

Prayers on our behalf to Christ by either saints living in heaven, or friends living on earth would, again, be called *secondary mediation*.

Prayers on our behalf to Christ by either saints living in heaven, or friends living on earth would, again, be called secondary mediation.

St. Paul talks about this throughout his epistles, like in Romans 15:30-32; Colossians 1:4, 9-10; and 2 Corinthians 1:10. Additionally, check out Romans 10:1; and 2 Timothy 1:3.

Saints Alive!

The saints in heaven are alive and are perpetually in prayer. They are absolutely living in heaven, just as you and I live, but to an even fuller extent, because they are back home with God. He is "the God of the living, not of the dead" (Mark 12:26-27).

Since they are far closer to God than we are (2 Corinthians 3:18), as sinful humans walking the earth, their prayers are more powerful.

The saints in heaven are free of all sin, which is what hinders our prayers (Matthew 17:20; 1 John 3:22; Psalms 66:18) and they are in total, perfect union with God.

We honor Mary and the saints not because they desire it, but because they deserve it.

We are still united with our saintly brothers and sisters (1 Corinthians 12:21-27; Romans 12:5; Ephesians 4:4; Colossians 3:15), as "death cannot separate us from Christ" (Romans 8:35-39).

Again, the Mother of our Lord prophesied that "all generations will call me blessed" (Luke 1:48). No other faith on earth fulfills this prophecy with the degree of faithfulness that the Catholic Church does. We honor Mary and the saints not because they desire it, but because *they deserve it*...they "ran the race" well and received their "crown of righteousness" (1 Corinthians 9:24-25; 2 Timothy 2:11-12; 4:7).

May our Mother Mary and all the saints and angels, pray for us!

SUGGESTED READING:
Hebrews 12:1, 12:18-19, 12:22-24;
Revelation 5:8, 14; 6:10, 8:3-4.
The Staff of Catholic Answers, *The Essential Catholic Survival Guide*
Fr. Mario Romero, *Unabridged Christianity*
Frank Sheed, *Theology for Beginners*
Fr. Robert Barron, *Catholicism*, Chapter IV

QUESTION 58

DO CATHOLICS WORSHIP STATUES?

IN BRIEF:

Once, while browsing a Christian bookstore, I came across a book that supposedly "exposed" all kinds of heretical and "anti-Biblical" teachings of the Catholic faith. It was astounding how something so poorly researched and historically inaccurate could be published. One section, in particular, on how Catholics "worship statues" was just painful to read – it was a true celebration of ignorance. Unfortunately, as with most misconceptions, these conclusions are drawn with little or no true understanding of the Catholic faith or of the practice in question.

If the author had asked me, "Do you, as a Catholic, believe worshipping a statue is wrong?" I would have replied in a resounding, "Yes. Of course worshipping a statue is wrong."

The Roman Catholic Church teaches that statue worship would be wrong, just as God revealed and Scripture echoes:

> *"You shall not carve idols for yourselves in the shape of anything in the sky above or on the earth below or in the waters beneath the earth; you shall not bow down before them or worship them."*
> - Exodus 20:4-5

The question is not whether or not worshipping an idol or – in this case – a statue is wrong, the question is when prayer becomes worship and when a visual aid becomes an idol.

IN DEPTH:

Many Christians are shocked to learn that there are several places in the Bible where God actually commands and "commissions" statues and images for religious usage:

- Exodus 25:10-22
- 1 Kings 6:23; 7:13-51
- Numbers 21:6-9
- Judges 17:1-6

Wait, but isn't God against idol worship? Is God sending two different messages here? No, not at all.

God ordered His children to construct these statues and images, but He did not intend for His children to worship them. God was using the images to help them to recall situations, to see places as holy and set apart, and to help them to open their minds and hearts and turn them back to God.

An image is not an idol. There is a difference.

An image is simply a spiritual 'visual aid' that is used by the faithful to increase their spirit of prayerfulness and devotion to God. An idol, on the other hand, is an image that is worshipped by the unfaithful in place of the one true God (i.e., the 'golden calf' described in Exodus 32:7-8).

God ordered His children to construct these statues and images, but He did not intend for His children to worship them.

In the Old Testament, images of God were forbidden because people had not yet seen God in human form. In the New Testament, God has taken on human form...an image that we can see.

"He (Jesus) is the image of the invisible God [...]"
- Colossians 1:15

In the Old Testament, images of God were forbidden because people had not yet seen God in human form. In the New Testament, God has taken on human form...an image that we can see.

This point is further illuminated in passages like John 14:9, Colossians 2:9, and 1 John 1:1-2, just to name a few.

When we profess that Jesus Christ is Lord, we must remember that we are professing the Incarnation. That is, that God became flesh – the One who we could see, smell, hear, touch, and (through the Eucharist) taste!

When we look upon a statue as we meditate in prayer to God, our senses are illuminated. We are not worshipping the wood, plaster, plastic, or paint. The image, though, appeals to our sense of sight, aiding in our visualization and helping us to focus on the pure, consistent, and holy life lived by that saint...like the Blessed Virgin Mary, for instance.

Here are a few more things to keep in mind:

- Stained glass windows with images can work in the same way... but most people don't seem to have a problem with those, because "they're just pretty." Images were very important in the early times of our Church's history, especially when many of the faithful were illiterate and could not read the word of God on their own. The images helped them recall instances and situations in the Word that they had heard about, but could not read on their own.

- If any of your Christian friends (non-Catholic) display a Nativity set during Advent and Christmas are they accused of worshiping idols?

- We put framed pictures of loved ones on mantles and walls of our homes, but that doesn't mean that we worship them...or the wooden frame or its glass.

- The weatherman uses a visual aid of maps when forecasting the weather, but couldn't he just tell us the facts and read the temperatures?

- Is a children's picture Bible that includes animations and drawings throughout it, the worshipping of images? Those are images, too.

Finally, consider this last thought regarding what the early Christians did:

> *"Previously God, who has neither a body nor a face, absolutely could not be represented by an image. But now that He has made Himself visible in the flesh and has lived with men, I can make an image of what I have seen of God...and contemplate the glory of the Lord, His face unveiled."*
> — St. John Damascene [749 AD]

SUGGESTED READING:

CCC 1159-62, 2131, 2705
Fr. Robert Barron, *Catholicism*
The Staff of Catholic Answers, *The Essential Catholic Survival Guide*
Dale Ahlquist, *Common Sense 101: Lessons from G. K. Chesterton*
Scott Hahn, *The Lamb's Supper*

WHAT MAKES SOMEONE A SAINT?

IN BRIEF:

A statue, a holy card, some stained glass and a heck of a lot of "Hail Marys."

Okay, that was stupid.

While earthly titles and personal resumes may matter to employers, they do not matter to God. In fact, the only "title" God cares about for us is that we are His son or daughter. Beyond that, the only earthly "title" that would leave heaven applauding would be that of a "saint."

To be clear, the Church doesn't "make someone" a saint. The Church recognizes the holiness of certain individuals and honors some with the title of "saint." If you make it to heaven, you are a saint – whether or not the Church recognizes you as one publicly.

IN DEPTH:

The title of saint is conferred on someone after what is called the canonization process. The process was most formalized by Pope Alexander III in the 12th century. He restricted the prerogative of canonization to the Holy See (Vatican authority), meaning that the Church was the body that would officially declare someone a "saint," and not just their local community or country.

> **Canonization means 'being raised to the full honors of the altar.' You can read more about this in the Catechism of the Catholic Church (828).**

Canonization means 'being raised to the full honors of the altar.' You can read more about this in the *Catechism of the Catholic Church* (828).

So nowadays, for instance, say that you had someone you wanted to suggest for sainthood. Here are the "steps" that would need to occur for that person to receive the "title":

- You and a group would send a report to the Congregation for the Causes of Saints (a Vatican group).

- That Congregation would research the candidate's virtues and life to see if the person should be recommended or not.

- The aforementioned report is then reviewed by the Holy Father. If the Pope accepts the report from the Congregation, the person in question is titled Venerable. Venerable means "accorded great respect due to heroic character."

- Once venerable, there are several more steps in the process in which the person's life is exhaustively researched and examined. If alive, witnesses are contacted who knew the deceased. Various people can come forward to raise objections. Debates can ensue and long discussions can be had.

- Also, at least one miracle must occur and be directly attributed to that saint's intercession to God. Once that happens (if and when it does), the person is "beatified" in a ceremony by the pope at St. Peter's in Rome and declared Blessed.

> *He's given us the sacraments to ensure we become holy and the saints to offer a model of life and example of prayer. The only thing missing is your consent to allow the Holy Spirit to make you a saint.*

- After a period of time and another two miracles the "Blessed" will be recommended for canonization and named a saint at a ceremony in Rome (although there have been some canonization ceremonies that took place outside of the Vatican – like in Korea in 1984).

Whether your life is ever investigated or a statue ever chiseled, the good news is that God has given us every opportunity to become saints in our everyday life. He's given us the Sacraments to ensure we become holy and the saints to offer a model of life and example of prayer. The only thing missing is your consent to allow the Holy Spirit to make you a saint.

Your sainthood doesn't begin when a council starts investigating your life. Your invitation to sainthood began at your Baptism. Your life – right now – is your RSVP. Just live today and every day for heaven and let your resume take care of itself.

SUGGESTED READING:

CCC 828, 946-62, 2030
Fr. Robert Barron, *Catholicism*
Alan Schreck, *The Compact History of the Catholic Church*
The Staff of Catholic Answers, *The Essential Catholic Survival Guide*
Life Teen, *Holier Than Thou*

WHY DO CATHOLICS BELIEVE IN THE ASSUMPTION?

IN BRIEF:

I was once asked, "Why do you Catholics believe that Mary ascended into heaven when it's not even in the Bible?"

"Well, first . . . " I replied, "Mary did not ascend into heaven; the Blessed Virgin Mary was assumed into heaven. Jesus ascended by His own power. Mary was taken up into heaven by God." That little difference is a big difference, so I wanted to be sure the young man understood it.

The young man then asserted, "Well, that (the Assumption of Mary) couldn't happen."

I responded, "Did not happen, or could not happen?" Again, the difference is huge.

It's one thing to say that Mary "didn't" get assumed into heaven but to say that Mary could not would be anti-Scriptural, as others in the Bible were, in fact, carried off to heaven. We will talk about why the Church holds firm to this dogmatic teaching (dogmatic means "incontrovertibly true").

Words matter. Details matter. And, remember, not everything that we believe comes directly from written tradition (as we heard about on page 84). The Tradition of Mary's Assumption, though not "officially" clarified until 1950, was the commonly understood belief from the early Church. Now, let's talk in greater depth about why the Church knows this to be true.

IN DEPTH:

First, we need to be certain that Mary even died. I mean, Scripture doesn't tell us that she died. So let's begin there.

Did Mary Die?

Maybe Mary didn't die. Maybe she's living in Brazil . . . next door to Elvis. Some people point to the fact that only Elijah and Enoch are mentioned as being carried off to heaven in Scripture, and since Mary is not, then "it must not be true."

Have you ever noticed that although the Acts of the Apostles is an incredibly detailed accurate account of Sts. Peter and Paul, we do not read of their deaths on the pages of Scripture? Everything we know of their deaths comes from early oral tradition. In fact, the Bible doesn't say what happened to most of the disciples. The Bible is silent in this area. Many Evangelicals accept the witness of Church history that Saint Peter was crucified upside-down in Rome, that Paul was beheaded, etc. — even though Scripture does not record these events.

We know from oral tradition that Mary was taken into the care of St. John (the writer of the fourth Gospel and the Book of Revelation) and went to live with him in Ephesus (where he was a Bishop). We know that she was sought out for her counsel and wisdom, and that she was exalted and honored throughout the community. Early Church Tradition upholds these facts as true, as do historic and non-canonical writings.

What is different, though, is that we know where the bones of Sts. Peter and Paul and other disciples like Mary Magdalene are because the early Christians took care of them. There is no record of where the bones of Mary are. It seems a little odd that if there had been a body no one would have given her a proper burial or that her tomb would not have become a landmark, does it not?

How Do We Know Mary is in Heaven?
Well, if the woman who God specifically chose to bring His Son into the world and raise Him is not in heaven, none of us have a shot.

Seriously though, is there Scriptural backing for this teaching about the Assumption? Absolutely! While it does not explicitly state, "Mary was assumed into heaven" in the Bible, stop and take a look at the verses from Revelation (written by John) of visions that were seen:

> *"Then God's temple in heaven was opened, and the ark of His covenant could be seen in the temple. There were flashes of lightning, rumblings, and peals of thunder, an earthquake, and a violent hailstorm. A great sign appeared in the sky, a woman clothed with the sun, with the moon under her feet, and on her head a crown of twelve stars. She was with child and wailed aloud in pain as she labored to give birth. She gave birth to a son, a male child, destined to rule all the nations with an iron rod... Then I heard a loud voice in heaven say: "Now have salvation and*

power come, and the Kingdom of our God and the authority of His Anointed.'"

- Revelation 11:19, 12:1-6, 10

This revelation is referring to Mary in heaven. Mary is often referred to as the new "Ark of the Covenant."

You may have seen images of "the Ark of the Covenant" in a study Bible or in old movies like "Raiders of the Lost Ark" with Indiana Jones. The Ark of the Old Covenant contained the Ten Commandments (the Law), a pot of manna (heavenly bread) and the staff of Aaron (symbol of Priesthood). You can read about the Ark – but not Indiana Jones – in Hebrews 9:4. The Ark was kept free from all defect and corruption, made from the finest most pure materials to God's exact specifications.

As the Ark of the New Covenant, Mary carried Christ who is the Law, the Bread of Life, and the Royal High Priest. Her Immaculate Conception and her state as ever-virgin kept her free from both defect and sin, preserving her throughout her life until her death where she was immediately assumed to preserve her from any bodily corruption on earth. Notice, too, in this passage from Revelation that we see the Ark (which is missing on earth) in heaven immediately preceding our vision of this woman crowned in stars and holding a baby. To whom did God give this vision (Revelation)? He imparted it to St. John, the one who was entrusted with caring for our Mother, Mary (John 19:25-27) for the remainder of her days on earth prior to her Assumption.

In 1950, Pope Pius XII defined the doctrine of the Assumption of the Blessed Virgin Mary for the universal Church. The teaching was not new, only now formally clarified.

History Gave Us Her Story.
In 1950, Pope Pius XII defined the doctrine of the Assumption of the Blessed Virgin Mary for the universal Church. The teaching was not new, only now formally clarified. He affirmed that at the end of her time on earth, Mary experienced immediately the resurrection of the body that is promised to all faithful followers of Jesus.

Basically, since Mary was preserved from original sin by the unique gift of Christ's grace, she was able to experience the immediate perfect union with her Son in heaven, never knowing or suffering from bodily corruption or decay (due to death) in any way.

Remember, as Christians we believe in the resurrection of the body. As the Papal encyclical *Lumen Gentium* (68) asserts, Mary's assumption and heavenly presence preceded and foreshadows our own future glory (1 Corinthians 15). You might want to check out how the *Catechism of the Catholic Church* explains it, too (*CCC* 966).

Remember, as Christians we believe in the resurrection of the body. As the Papal encyclical Lumen Gentium (68) asserts, Mary's assumption and heavenly presence preceded and foreshadows our own future glory .

One of the things that sets us apart from other Christian denominations is that we have a rich understanding of Mary and a tradition of giving her the honor she deserves. She can teach us a lot through her example of virtue and her special role within the Church. Pray with Mary and she will lead you into a far deeper relationship with her Son than you could ever achieve by your own direction.

Hail Mary!

SUGGESTED READING:

CCC 966
Fulton Sheen, *The World's First Love*
Scott Hahn, *Hail Holy Queen: The Mother of God in the Word of God*
Pope Benedict XVI, *Mary: The Church at the Source*
Fr. Mario Romero, *Unabridged Christianity*
The Staff of Catholic Answers, *The Essential Catholic Survival Guide*